BECAUSE THIS IS TEXAS

PRAISE

*"Learned journals, as a rule,
are unexciting and opposite of sexy, but
(this) will knock your hat in the creek."*
KENT BIFFLE,
The Dallas Morning News

*"One of the great Amarillo
stories—some say the greatest—told
with authority and high style."*
MARY KAYE TRIPP,
Amarillo Globe-News

PRAISE FOR BEFORE WE TURN TO DUST

*"A fresh new voice in literary fiction
steps onto the stage."*
JODI THOMAS
New York Times bestselling author

BECAUSE THIS IS TEXAS

AN ACCOUNT OF THE SNEED-BOYCE FEUD

CLARA SNEED

For information, address:
Blue Handle Publishing
2067 Wolflin Ave. #963
Amarillo, TX 79109

For information about bulk, educational,
and other special discounts, please contact
Blue Handle Publishing,
www.BlueHandlePublishing.com.

To book Clara Sneed for any event,
contact Blue Handle Publishing.

Cover and interior design:
Blue Handle Publishing

Editing: Book Puma Author Services,
BookPumaEdit.com

ISBN: 978-1-955058-30-8

To Albert "Pete" Boyce and Joe Pool.

*They left this world and
this book much better off.*

CONTENTS

NOTE TO THE READER

From Ricky Treon, director of publishing
Blue Handle Publishing

This true story of passion and vengeance (and restraint, believe it or not) has been told and retold orally and in periodicals since the events first took place more than a century ago.

And the following isn't even the first time this version of the story has been in print. "Because This is Texas: An Account of the Sneed-Boyce Feud" by Clara Sneed originally appeared in the pages of the *Panhandle-Plains Historical Review* in 1999.

But alongside this nonfiction account of her family's history, Clara was working on a fictionalized version. Her novel would put readers inside the heads of this epic love triangle's principal players, exploring much more deeply the complex emotions and legal machinations.

That wonderful literary novel is called *Before We Turn to Dust*, and I'm proud to say Blue Handle Publishing released it in hardcover in late 2024. And because it was so closely based on true events, we were excited to also release the nonfiction account in book form. We wanted to fill in gaps for those who wanted more information about the story, and to read more about what happened after the novel's narrative ends, including how the events rippled through to the modern era.

We also loved the story so much that we wanted the nonfiction account to get its full due and reach as many readers as possible.

The following has not been revised from how it originally appeared in the *Panhandle Plains Historical Review*, except for cosmetic changes to adhere to standard book formatting and copy rules.

We hope you enjoy it and get the rest of the story—not to mention some facts not included here—by savoring the pages of *Before We Turn to Dust*, if you haven't already.

From Clara Sneed, author
and Sneed family descendant (1999)

Only the generous help of many people made possible the writing of this account. Ferreting out the details in a dramatic story such as this one necessitates acts of kindness from strangers, friends, and family. Though I am indebted to all, I should like to single out for particular mention a few.

Mary Kate Tripp, book editor and columnist for the *Amarillo Globe-News*, edited a book which Thomas Thompson, former editor of the paper, wrote on this subject in the 1980s. That book now rests in the Panhandle-Plains Historical Society Archives, unpublished and, because of the terms of Thompson's will, inaccessible for a number of years.

Mrs. Tripp served not only as Thompson's editor, but also as his friend and sounding board, roles she has also generously filled for me. Through her, I have had access to some of the information Thompson gathered that might otherwise have escaped me.

I have been fortunate also in the assistance of the Amarillo Public Library, and in particular of Katie Anthony, who tirelessly tracked down books and information.

In addition, my cousin, Joe Pool, has opened his voluminous files to me, providing some of Beal Sneed's correspondence and other source material.

Perhaps my greatest debt, however, is to A. G. Boyce's great-grandson and A. G. Boyce Jr.'s great-nephew, yet another Albert G. Boyce. He was willing to share relevant correspondence that has survived in his family's archives.

Newspaper accounts, in particular those of the *Fort Worth Star-Telegram*; a habeas corpus hearing transcript; and the Boyce correspondence, form the major source material for the account that follows.[1]

KEY CITIES

CLAYTON, N.M.
• DALHART
• CHANNING
AMARILLO

SANTA ROSA, N.M.

CHILDRESS •

• PADUCAH

LUBBOCK

• PLANO
FORT WORTH DALLAS

MIDLAND

• EL PASO
ODESSA   ABILENE

• WACO

GEORGETOWN • CALVERT

★
AUSTIN
HOUSTON •

SAN ANTONIO

TEXAS
• LAREDO

PROLOGUE

In 1912, the Red Sox won the World Series and Jim Thorpe won Olympic gold in the pentathlon and decathlon. It was the last year in which Americans faced no income tax. Fashionable women wore hobble skirts while English suffragettes bombed the home of Lloyd George. The unsinkable Titanic sank. In Lawrence, Massachusetts, textile workers went on strike, and militiamen were called out to quell the disturbance. Congress investigated working conditions in steel mills. Alfred Adler published *The Neurotic Constitution*; those who treated diseases of the mind were termed "alienists." Vaslav Nijinsky danced *Afternoon of a Faun*, Edgar Rice Burroughs published *Tarzan of the Apes*, and Marcel Duchamp exhibited the controversial "Nude Descending a Staircase." Woodrow Wilson, William Howard Taft, and Theodore Roosevelt, all Progressives, contended for the American presidency with little awareness that, a scant two years later, rumblings in the Balkans would provoke a catastrophe from which their nation would not escape. In 1912, America was a world "betwixt and between": A world still emerging from the long reach of Victorianism, not yet engulfed in the epoch-defining disaster of World War I.

In 1912, in the panhandle of Texas, the famed XIT Ranch, created in the mid-1880s out of three million acres of public land given in exchange for building the state capitol in Austin, sold the last of its once-vast herds;[2] it was the age of the nester, rather than of cattle empires. And on the evening of January 13, 1912, the XIT's former longtime manager, "Colonel" Albert G. Boyce, then almost seventy, sat chatting in the lobby of Fort Worth's premier hotel, the Metropolitan.[3] Rushing through the hotel's revolving doors, hat pulled low, a man half the Colonel's age pulled a .32 caliber handgun from beneath his coat and fired at the old man five or six times. Boyce died within the hour. Nine months later, on September 14, 1912, the same man gunned down Boyce's son and namesake, Albert G. Boyce Jr., as he strolled down Polk Street in Amarillo. Al, as he was usually known, died almost instantly, face resting in the grass beside the Polk Street Methodist Church.[4] The killer was my great-uncle, John Beal Sneed.

I have heard this story all my life, though frequently in a garbled form, sometimes simplified so that Beal—as he was called—killed only one man, the man the story demanded that he kill. In 1912, the murders and the events that led up to them were hugely newsworthy in Texas and elsewhere. But by the time I was born forty years later, the tale had passed into the realm of detail-blurring, mostly hushed-tone discussion, at least by the generation contemporary to it. In the 1950s, one of the chroniclers of XIT history, Louis Nordyke, tried to write a book about the saga and had to give up: no one would talk to him.[5] C. L. Sonnichsen, in his book about Texas feuding, *I'll Die Before I'll Run*, had also recognized that it was "too soon."[6] While the "Boyce-Sneed affair," as Sonnichsen characterized it, was not a feud in the classic sense—largely because of the Boyces's admirable restraint—it certainly was a feud in all but the classic sense. It divided the families involved and the Amarillo community for decades. Thus, the Sonnichsen analysis of the silence that surrounded feuds is applicable.

A few years ago, I began researching the story for myself. Unfortunately, many of those contemporary to the events have passed on, leaving certain mysteries which at this time I have been unable to resolve—though many of the dead might not have talked even if they could have. The tale is the old one of a triangle: of a love affair of such enormous heat and passion that it blinded the lovers to any mere commonsense concerns, and of a marriage which ultimately survived adultery and two murders. And it is, undoubtedly, a Texas story, evidencing the survival of the values of the Old West and the Old South, as well as the challenges and changes the twentieth century had brought to those values.

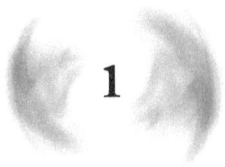

1

John Beal Sneed and Lenora Snyder married in 1900 in Georgetown, Texas, and shortly thereafter moved to Childress.[7] Beal was the son of Joseph Tyre Sneed Sr., a wealthy cattleman and farmer. Lena, as Lenora Snyder Sneed was known, was the daughter of Thomas Shelton Snyder and the niece of J. W. and D. H. Snyder, the well-known cattlemen and trail drivers.[8] Beal and Lena moved to Amarillo in 1904.[9] Colonel Boyce retired from managing the XIT in 1905 and also moved to town with his family.[10]

The earlier generations of Sneeds, Snyders, and Boyces had lived through the defeat of the Confederacy and had remade their lives after the Civil War, becoming wealthy and respected in the process. The Snyders and the Boyces had known each other in Round Rock, where Colonel Boyce had courted his wife, Annie,[11] and Tom Snyder had seen the legendary Texas outlaw Sam Bass after he collapsed from Ranger gunfire under a live oak tree on D. H. Snyder's property.[12] Colonel Boyce had driven cattle for the Snyder brothers; in fact, he was driving a Snyder herd to stock the XIT when he first visited the ranch.[13]

Beal's father, Joe Sneed Sr., owned property in Milam and Falls counties, also in Central Texas.[14]

Later, the Snyder, Sneed, and Boyce families had moved to Georgetown, where Beal and Lena and Al spent time together in their youth. All three attended Southwestern University, though Lena and Al, as was then often the case with ranchers' children, did not graduate.[15] Lena probably followed a course of study appropriate for well-bred young women of the period. Beal, on the other hand, was intellectually gifted and went on to graduate from the University of Texas and to take a law degree at Princeton University.[16]

In 1904, when Beal and Lena moved to Amarillo, it was a town of two thousand people. By 1910, however, it had grown into a thriving city of fifteen thousand, if one included the "suburbs."[17] The Queen City of the Plains was full of contrasts and contradictions. Streetcars ran on streets for the most part not yet paved.[18] You could ride one out to Glenwood, where there was an amusement park with a roller coaster and an automobile in which you could pose for a photo. Downtown, the Opera House drew patrons, but so did the Bowery, a rough and ready district about to be shut or at least slowed down by local prohibition. Ministers spent many a sermon railing against the evils of alcohol, but the town drank hard, and when the "drys" campaigned for their initiatives, they frequently put men in the speakers' podium whom everybody knew to be drinkers.[19] Each Sunday, the churches filled, as they do to this day. The town's raison d'etre was cattle shipping: there were massive holding pens, and a large transient population of cowboys drifting in with the herds, spending all their money in the Bowery, and drifting out again. At the top of the social heap sat the wealthy cattlemen, gossiping and making their deals in the lobby of the Amarillo Hotel.[20]

The city sat on mostly bare plains, though a few tiny trees had been planted, primarily in front of the massive homes built by prosperous cattlemen and bankers. The standard Amarillo home for the wealthy at the time was of brick or stone or occasionally wood, often with a dormered half story sitting like a Cyclops's eye over a heavy-pillared front porch. Termed "bungalows," these houses were substantial in their effect, as if daring the plains—so long unoccupied except by the buffalo, Comanche, Kiowa, occasional Mexican pastores, and Comancheros—to ignore or belittle the house's occupants. The Boyces had one such house at 1104 Polk Street.[21] Beal and Lena had another, one block west and three blocks south at 1500 Tyler Street.[22]

By 1910, Beal and Lena had apparently lived harmoniously enough as husband and wife for ten years. They had two daughters, Lenora and Georgia Beal. The well-to-do family enjoyed whatever amenities Amarillo had to offer, benefiting from electric lights and telephones and automobiles and all the other new-fangled

3

conveniences for the wealthy, and generally behaving in a socially acceptable manner. No one had anything for which to reproach Lena beyond a certain "wildness" that was very attractive in many cases. Vivacious and likable, she was a lot of fun, noted for the parties she gave for Amarillo ladies in broad daylight, with the shades drawn and candles blazing inside. Reportedly, the neighbors enjoyed her, with one caveat: you did not want to lend her anything unless you were prepared to retrieve it. Somehow or other, she just never seemed to remember to return that ice cream maker or that extra set of dessert spoons.[23] Her husband appeared upright enough and materially indulgent of his wife and daughters—a point that was repeatedly emphasized by witnesses at his trials, cited as sufficient proof, in most cases, of his kindness as a husband, and underlining an assumed connection between being a "good provider" and other less-tangible qualities. He was a relatively successful cattleman and farmer,[24] absent from home about two-thirds of the time because of his business interests.[25]

Amarillo was a handy place for cattlemen to headquarter their families when business called, as it frequently did. The city offered proximity to their land and social and educational amenities for their wives and children. Lena was, no doubt, used to absent males. Due to their ranching interests, her father and uncles must have been away from home frequently.[26] Nevertheless, the old stories indicate that Beal neglected Lena, as many cattlemen appeared to neglect their wives.[27] Mrs. Tripp and I have had numerous conversations on the subject of Lena's and Beal's marriage; she has made this point frequently in the course of them.

In the fall of 1910, Al Boyce Jr. returned to Amarillo. He and his brother Lynn had ranched in Montana, but Al had moved to the Pecos after the two bought another ranch there, leaving Lynn to close down their Montana operation. Due to a drought, Al shipped some of the Pecos cattle into Amarillo. He returned with them and subsequently made the Boyce home on Polk Street his headquarters, occasionally visiting the Pecos ranch and other places where he and Lynn had interests.[28] Despite the families' intimacy, it seems likely that Al and Lena had not seen much of each other since her marriage. They had been in different places too much of the time.

There has always been speculation—starting from the initial newspaper coverage of the story—that Al and Lena had been serious sweethearts as teenagers. "Pathetic Story of Schoolday Love of Two Men for Same Girl, Hate and Revenge, Revealed in Boyce-Sneed Tragedies" trumpeted the headline of the *Fort Worth Star-Telegram* on September 15, 1912, the day after Al's death. "Threads of pathos and tragedy, of a love that time and the unrelenting hand of fate could not lessen, are woven into the life history of Lena Sneed . . . John Beal

Sneed, and Al Boyce Jr." began the sidebar story. In Georgetown, the story continued, Lena had "smiled with the careless freedom of a schoolgirl upon those who sought her favor . . . yielding at last to the pleadings of John Beal Sneed. . . . Al Boyce, who had been one of her most ardent suitors, passed out of her life."

Another version of the tale, surviving in gossip rather than in newspaper accounts, paints Lena as the spurned woman. In this scenario, she married Beal on the rebound after her romance with Al was broken up when the Colonel summoned his family to ranch headquarters in Channing, where he put all of them to work for the XIT, eventually appointing Al as assistant manager.[29] Thomas Thompson firmly believed this scenario. Mrs. Tripp, however, does not: "I just don't see her as the type of woman who would have let a man go if she was really interested in him."[30]

Tom Snyder Sr. and Beal both denied that there had been any attachment prior to that which arose after Al returned to Amarillo in 1910.[31] Snyder claimed that Lena was "12 or 13 years old when the Boyces left Georgetown. She and Al Boyce Jr. were never sweethearts."[32] The date of the Boyce family move to Channing is not entirely clear. Possibly, Al returned from Channing to attend Southwestern, and there encountered Lena again when both were older.[33] In the surviving lovers' letters, however, neither mention any previous relationship.[34] Yet the lack of anything formal or specific would not have precluded a general attraction to one another, never really acknowledged or acted upon, but never really forgotten, either. Such a history might go a long way to explain the kind of fierce purity of their feelings when they became lovers as adults. Their letters strike one as possessed of a kind of intensity and a level of devotion that is often characteristic of first loves.

Al's photograph, taken in an earlier, happier time at the XIT headquarters in Channing, reveals a darkly handsome young man, with a kind of sexual, brooding quality to his face. Feet resting on the lobo wolf skins scattered over the floor, lips slightly parted, he is holding a banjo as he stares at the camera, unsmiling (as was the convention of the time) and alert, a seeming subtle challenge at play in his features. The photo makes it easy to believe the claim of a number of witnesses that once he'd made up his mind he could not be budged.

Between Al's image and Lena's, in a photo probably taken around 1910, there seems, not a family resemblance exactly, but a kind of mirroring effect—his dark eyes echoed by her own, both pairs hinting at depths at once dangerous and inviting.

Beal's photos, on the other hand, portray a man of a different sort: somewhat stocky, balding, and forceful, if not aggressive, in appearance; very much the *pater familias*, with perhaps a deep and unexpressed sorrow submerged in his eyes. If one lines the three photos up together,

Lenora "Lena" Sneed at about forty.
Photo from the author's collection.

Albert G. Boyce Sr., general manager of the XIT Ranch, 1887-1905. *Photograph courtesy of the XIT Museum, Dalhart, Texas.*

he seems very much the odd man out; Al and Lena, in the common expression, look like "they belong together."

Regardless of whether she harbored suppressed feelings for Al, however, when Lena married Beal in 1900, he must have looked like a good catch. He was a lawyer, he had attended Princeton University, he came from a good family and his prospects seemed bright. Nonetheless, by the fall of 1910, at age thirty-one, her views had changed. Beal was thirty-two. Al was thirty-four.[35]

According to Beal's testimony, the relationship between Al and Lena began, or resumed, over trading books; "[Al] would come up there to get books to read and my wife, I think at his mother's suggestions, brought down books for him to read. She would come up and get them sometimes, and he would come up and get them sometimes."[36]

Popular novels of the time—such as Zane Gray's *Riders of the Purple Sage*, Owen Wister's *The Virginian*, and Harold Bell Wright's *The Winning of Barbara Worth* and *The Shepherd of the Hills*—all deal with love in the sentimental style of the era. Wright occasionally resorts to italicizing the word *mate* to suggest the weighty import of uniting with the right person.[37] Whatever happened in the fall and winter after Al returned to Amarillo, it seems to have included Lena's and Al's growing recognition that they were mates. In May of 1911, they became lovers.[38] Wright and the other authors all heartily applauded finding

10

John Beal Sneed and his daughters, Georgia Beal, left, and Lenora. Circa 1910. *Photograph from the author's collection.*

oneself the right mate, but they did not cover the contingency that Al and Lena now faced: What do you do if one of you has already chosen the wrong one?

What Lena chose to do set in motion all subsequent events. On October 13, 1911, Beal came home about eleven-thirty to have an early dinner, planning later to take some men "out to the ranch to show them some cattle that day."[39] Lena sent the children in to eat and informed him she had something to tell him.

[S]he took me out on the front gallery, sat down in a swing on the gallery and proceeded to tell me about this infatuation for this man, she told me she had decided to go to South America with this man, and live the rest of her life with him, and take the children. She says, 'He wanted me to go without saying anything to you about it, but I wanted to tell you. I knew that you would be willing for me to go, and either let me take both of the children or take one of the children, if you would not let me take them both.' I, of course—looking back at it today—I did not, could not believe, could not realize what she was saying, and she probably repeated it to me two or three times. Finally, I said to her, 'What in the world are you talking about?' . . . I finally realized she was serious about the matter. Of course, she repeated it a number of times—told me she never loved me in her life. She was willing to leave her children if I would not let her take them with her. She never cared for anything in the world but this man and was going away with him and live with him the rest of her life.[40]

This theme of Lena "never having loved" a person to whom she had previously been closely attached recurred in Beal's testimony. He claimed that, after her father's and sister's arrival in Amarillo to aid in the marital crisis, Lena chided them, saying, "You have turned against me. I hate you, I hate my mother, I hate all of you—you have hated me all of your life. I don't want to ever see any of you. I wish you had not come down here. I did not want you here."[41]

The foregoing account is the commonly accepted version of how Beal became aware of the affair. And it may be the true one. But there is enough evidence to suggest something more complex, possibly suppressed in part due to contemporary restrictions on what could be printed in the newspapers,[42] and in part because it was in the defense's interest to present the story as Beal recounted it—an innocently happy husband suddenly becoming aware of his wife's infidelity.

According to the Sneed family physician, Dr. R. L. McMeans, Lena had been unwell during the summer and fall of 1911. Though her illness was never exactly specified, it had both physical and emotional manifestations: "She was nervous and run down and had been given a tonic. . . . [A] month or six weeks before [she] was brought to Fort Worth . . . [McMeans] told Sneed that if he didn't take her to the sea coast or some low place in a reasonable time, she might lose her mind."[43]

Beal testified that when he'd returned home

one day about two weeks prior to Lena's confession on October 13—about the end of September 1911—he'd discovered Al holding her hand as she rested in bed. Lena's excuse for this behavior was that her nails were blue, and she was showing them to Al. Beal agreed that they were indeed "right purple or blue," and claimed he bought her story. She had been sick "a couple of weeks."[44]

Not long before this episode, about mid-September, the elder Boyces evidently became deeply alarmed at the course of things between Lena and Al. They took Al to New Orleans, hoping that a doctor who had helped the ailing Colonel regain his strength during the previous year might cure Al of his infatuation. Al refused to go without Lena's permission, which she gave; nevertheless, Al was back in Amarillo by the end of the month.[45]

A Sneed neighbor, Mrs. S. A. Morris, testified that about the same time—mid-September—she first discovered the "misconduct" when Lena, whom Morris described as "nervous and suffering from female troubles,"[46] asked to use the Morris phone. As the Sneeds had a telephone, the request (which Morris denied)[47] suggests that Lena needed to make a call which could not be overheard at her own house.

Then around October 6, Al's brother, Henry, and Beal's brother, Joe, met in Dalhart to discuss the affair. They decided to "let the old men settle it," meaning Colonel Boyce, Tom Snyder, and J.T. Sneed Sr.[48] Joe was to wire Tom Snyder when he returned to Amarillo. According to Henry Boyce's testimony, however, Joe changed his mind on the train down and decided to wire his own father instead, an idea Henry thought a poor one since Beal and his father did not get along.[49] The two brothers also decided to send Joe with Al to Hot Springs, evidently hoping the waters, reputed to cure so much, would cure his passion.[50]

These incidents, taken together, suggest that concern over the relationship among those aware of it became heightened around September 1911. Testimony indicates that Lena's medical condition during the same time involved "female problems," nails that turned blue, and required a good deal of bed rest. Months later, on April 6, 1912, fretting to Al about the next trial, she wrote: "I feel like it would kill me to have it *all* in the papers again + oh precious there was so much that wasn't in the papers. All the facts about that miscarriage I had, came out—and that it was you—*you* don't know precious *you don't know*. Beal knew all the time."[51]

A miscarriage with substantial bleeding sometime in September 1911 might account for the blue nails Beal observed.[52] Although Lena, throughout her troubles, seemed to suffer from several symptoms we might now call psychosomatic, and Dr. McMeans' testimony suggests an emotional component to her illness, the blue nails are indisputably physical signs. A miscarriage, or a pregnancy for which Al was responsible, might also explain the increased concern on the part of Joe and Henry, as well as the elder Boyces.[53]

Lena's comment that "Beal knew all the time" is both intriguing and ambiguous. Mrs. Boyce stated on several occasions that Beal knew about the affair, or knew at least that Lena wanted a divorce, before he claimed to have discovered it.[54] There are also discrepancies between Beal's testimony and the testimony of Tom Snyder in this regard. Snyder testified several times that he arrived in Amarillo on October 12—the day before Beal said he found out—and that Beal informed him that his father had written him at Paducah telling him of the affair.[55] "Didn't you write to [Lena] from Paducah, while she was in Amarillo and after you had talked to your father, and ask her what she wanted to do about a separation?" asked one of the prosecutors during Beal's first trial. [56]

"I have no recollection of such a letter," was Beal's reported reply,[57] a very lawyerly denial indeed.

Beal's father, Joe Sneed Sr., testified that sometime between October 5 and October 10 he received a wire from his son-in-law, Terry Thompson, who was married to Beal's only sister, Georgia Sneed Thompson. That wire was no doubt a result of the discussion in Dalhart between Henry Boyce and Joe Sneed Jr. The elder Mr. Sneed went to the Thompson home in Amarillo, where he met with his daughter and Thompson, and also with Colonel Boyce, who came to the Thompson house to discuss the problem.[58] Dating the wire October 10 puts Mr. Sneed in Amarillo at a time that corresponds with Beal's testimony, while dating it October 5 puts him in town a week earlier, that is, prior to the time Beal testified he first heard of the affair from Lena. If Beal's father was in Amarillo a week before the scene on the gallery at the Sneed home, it seems possible that Beal knew about "the problem" before he claimed he did. But Beal also testified that Al warned Lena in the morning on October 13 that Mr. Sneed was in town and would be coming to tell Beal of the affair, meaning that his father knew the true situation before he did.[59]

On the other hand, nothing much was ever made of these discrepancies in chronologies or testimony. Both prosecution and defense, perhaps for opposite reasons, ultimately seem to have been happy to accept October 13, 1911, as the date Beal discovered his wife's passion for their childhood companion. The prosecution may have wanted to draw the veil of discretion over the fact that the Boyces were aware of the physical nature of the relationship between Al and Lena. Perhaps also they were afraid to risk alienating the jury if they attacked Beal on too many fronts. The defense, of course, did not want to explain an apparent earlier acceptance of the affair followed by Beal's explosions of violence.

Whether the truth differed significantly from the generally accepted version of the story is one of those mysteries likely to remain unsolved.

In any case, Beal's reaction to Lena's revelation on the thirteenth was dramatic. Late at night, after hours of talking and crying and sleeplessness, with Beal "wanting to know—trying to get her to give me some reason for this," he pulled out a gun. "I was so desperate, or wrought up, or was not myself, I do not know what—and I started to kill her— she grabbed hold of me, and trying to get her loose from me so I could kill her and then kill myself, she screamed several times, and the elder little girl ran in the room, and caught hold of the pistol and I put it up.[60]"

Many meetings among members of the three families took place about the second week in October. As has been noted, J. T. Sneed Sr. met with Colonel Boyce. Tom Snyder met with both the elder Boyces twice during his stay in Amarillo. On October 14, he also met with Henry Boyce for several hours on the train to Dalhart.[61] And Joe Sneed Sr. met with his son.

Beal testified that his father advised him to let Lena go: "Your wife has been false to you—a traitor to you, and there is not but one thing in the world you can do . . . throw her out and let her go." Beal responded to his father's counsel: "I knew it was not her—she could not realize what she wanted to do or was doing—that if she were herself, I knew she would be there pleading with her[self], trying to save her[self], instead of letting her[self] go, and that I owed it to her and her children, to try to stand by and protect her. And that I was going to do it to the end of the world."[62]

In his testimony, Beal persistently split Lena into two persons when explaining her behavior: she was "herself" when she was his good wife and the loving mother to their children; otherwise, she was, as it were, "possessed," dominated by her lover's influence, in the grip of something alien and insane. To portray Lena thus, or at least portray her husband as believing her thus, was part of the appeal of the defense strategy, a strategy that proved brilliantly successful.

Beal claimed Lena convinced him that there had been "no criminal intimacy" between her and Al, nothing but a few kisses, an opinion his father did not share.[63] Beal blamed the Boyce family for not having done anything to stop the relationship. After discussing the situation with his father, and with Tom Snyder and Lena's sister, Eula Snyder Bowman, Beal concluded that Lena, for whom he "was willing to do anything on earth that [he] could,"[64] should be committed. Accompanied by her children, father, husband, and sister, Lena boarded a train for Fort Worth. On October 17, 1911, her eleventh wedding anniversary, she was confined to the Arlington Heights Sanitarium.[65]

It was evidently quite simple at that time in Texas to commit one's problem relatives, particularly if the relative was one's wife.

Beal's word—in conjunction, obviously, with his pocketbook—was enough to ensure the cooperation of the Allison brothers, Wilmer and Bruce, who ran the Arlington Heights Sanitarium in a then-outlying area of Fort Worth. Over dinner at the Dallas Elks Club, Beal consulted Dr. John S. Turner, formerly superintendent of the state asylum at Terrell, about the case.[66] In the last part of October, Dr. Turner made several visits to observe and interview Lena. Initially, he declined to diagnose her as insane. After his second visit, he said he thought she was insane, but wanted to see her one more time to make certain. Eventually, the doctor decided she was suffering from "moral insanity."[67]

This diagnosis had been developed in the nineteenth century as a common, though controversial, means of categorizing behavior we would now call sociopathic or psychopathic: insanity, in other words, where the prevailing problem was a failure of the ethical or moral sense, rather than impairment of other faculties, as might be seen in a disease like schizophrenia. In Vienna in the 1870s, the term "moral insanity" was used to diagnose people whose deviations were primarily sexual and not otherwise definable.[68] The term's obvious imprecision and the subjective nature of its definition were later, in Lena's case, to provide much fodder for attorneys hoping to put Dr. Turner and the Allison brothers on the spot during cross-examination.

The Allisons and Dr. Turner believed it best that Lena be separated from her family, both husband and children. The children were taken to stay in Plano with Lena's sister, Eula, and her husband, Henry Bowman.[69] Beal was eager to see Lena, but was advised that although "she is your wife [and] you can see her whenever you want,"[70] it would be better if she were isolated from her loved ones. "I would rather see her than anybody else in the world," Beal testified he told Dr. Turner, "but my wishes and desires are not to be considered at all. I can walk on my heart for the rest of my life if it is for her good."[71]

After a few weeks, Dr. Turner believed Lena's condition had improved. Beal saw her briefly on October 30, claiming that during that visit she seemed more affectionate toward him than she had been for several months previously.[72] On November 6 and November 8, 1911, respectively, she wrote to him:

My dearest Beal . . . I was so disappointed over not seeing the children I felt like I couldn't stand it. Please talk about me to them every day and don't let them forget me. . . . Dr. Turner was over here yesterday, but of course you know this. I don't like him at all. . . . Don't think I am mad or hurt with you, for I am not, and I am trying so hard to believe you have done what is best for me, but it is mighty hard at times. . . . With lots of love & a million kisses for the babies. Your girl, Lena.

My dearest Beal . . . I was disappointed at not seeing you before you left, for there were so many things that

I wanted to know that nobody but you can tell me. You never said what the cattle brought nor what cotton was worth. . . . I know you have been so worried over the cattle & the cotton and I feel that I am to blame for it, and I am so sorry for it, and will try & be good to you and make up for it when I leave here. . . . I am almost crazy to see the children. . . . What did you do with the children's pony? & if Georgie [Thompson] wants to keep the cow you might let her have it, but I sure would lock the car up in the garage & not let anyone run it. . . . Please don't let [Dr. Turner] come anymore. He don't know anything about me as he don't stay over 15 min., and I believe I would have seen you and the children if it hadn't been for him. . . . I guess you will think to drain the radiators for if it should freeze they would break & ruin the floors. . . . If there is anything in my letter you miss, it is because I want to tell you instead of writing. Lovingly, Lena[73]

At the end of October, however, Lena had also written to Al. "For God's sake, come and take me away," she begged. Al received the letter in Santa Rosa, New Mexico, on November 2, and took the earliest train he could get to Fort Worth.[74] On November 8, after she wrote her second letter to Beal, Lena and her nurse, Lillie Flowers, went downtown, stopping to shop at a department store. From a large roll of money, Lena bought herself and Flowers some clothes.[75] Later, the two women met Al and Ed Farwell, assistant cashier at Dalhart's Midway Bank and Trust, of which Colonel Boyce was president and Henry Boyce the cashier.[76] All four went to the train station; two tickets were purchased; Al gave Lillie Flowers a check for five hundred dollars; and at seven-thirty that night, the lovers departed on the Frisco for St. Louis.[77] Testifying in the first Fort Worth trial for the murder of the Colonel (testimony that was stipulated to by the parties in Beal's habeas corpus hearing), the Frisco porter said that "during the night he heard Mrs. Lena Sneed crying and mourning, at said time. . . . Al Boyce was in said berth in said sleeper with her and that both of them were disrobed."[78] After that, until the end of December 1911, at least as far as Beal was concerned, his wife and her lover disappeared.

At this point in the story, while the principal parties are more or less offstage, it may be appropriate to offer some observations about the lovers' motivations. From the first, at least in his public declarations, Beal pictured his wife as a frail creature, easily led astray by Al and her own insanity. In his testimony, he claimed to want to care for her as one does a sick child.[79] Al was frequently pictured as a decadent, hard-drinking, chain-smoking seducer who thought nothing of destroying a happy home for his own nefarious and immoral purposes. Some attorneys implied that Lena was a "light" woman, as bad as or worse than a prostitute.[80] According to Lena's letters, all sorts of rumors were circulated about her. These ranged from speculation that she had a venereal disease to a report that she claimed was so awful she couldn't bring herself to write about it to Al: she did not understand what was meant when she first heard it.[81]

Four of Al's letters to Lena survive as exhibits attached to the Sneed habeas corpus hearing transcript. The bulk of the correspondence in the Boyce archives comprises letters from Lena to Al, extending from the end of December 1911 to August 10, 1912, about a month before his death. Judging from these letters, it is impossible to doubt the passion that the lovers felt for each other.

"My precious Lena,"[82] "My darling girl,"[83] are Al's typical salutations, echoed by Lena's "My own darling boy,"[84] and "My dear precious."[85]

"It nearly killed me the day they took you from me," wrote Al. "It hurt me worse than anything that ever happened to me. I was so broke up and cast down that I did not care what happened to me."[86]

"Life is one long aching pain away from you."[87]

"Life holds nothing for me precious but you, and I hope it will not be long [until you can procure a divorce] as it is only a weary hideous drag away from you. I love you so. . . . I love you and you are my very life. Your boy forever, Albert."[88]

Far from the cool exterior he reportedly showed to the world,[89] Al's letters reveal a passionate nature, almost boyish in its openness to his loved one.

Lena sounds equally impassioned. "Oh my absent boy," she wrote in a letter several weeks after the Colonel's murder, "I could write forever but I am afraid to—I am running a risk in mailing this, but I couldn't bear it any longer for you to be so far away with your aching heart + no word from your girl. . . . Oh, Albert, above everything say you love me + miss me + want me for I'm just living for you dear + to feel your arms around me once more + I pray God every night my precious boy to give you back to me for you are all that keeps me alive and I am your own girl thru this life and eternity."[90]

"I love you, love you, love you, and am your own girl," concludes another letter. "Look at your precious eyes + think how I love them."[91]

On occasion she signed her name as Lena Boyce[92] and promised "I am your own wife darling thru eternity."[93]

Lena's tone in the two letters written to Beal from the sanitarium is pallid by comparison. Taken as a whole, the lovers' correspondence suggests that beneath the adultery lay a kind of innocent trust in the strength of their feelings for each other and a doomed belief that the love between them was sufficient to reorder the world to permit them their happiness, regardless of what stood in the way.

After Al and Lena eloped, Beal spent a few days questioning nurse Lillie Flowers to get the true story. At one point, maddened by her obstinacy, he pulled a gun and threatened to shoot her. Terrified, she jumped out a ground floor sanitarium window, and the doctors intervened.[94] Once he discovered the truth, Beal hired the Burns Detective Agency to track the couple down,[95] supposedly spending $25,000 in the process.[96] On November 11, he succeeded in having a warrant issued for Al's arrest on state charges of abduction.[97] Trial testimony and Lena's letters indicate that the couple stopped in Chicago and Omaha, then crossed the border to Winnipeg.[98] On December 27, 1911, a few days after Beal was told they had been spotted in Canada, the *Manitoba Free Press* reported:

With the police of two countries searching for them, and a reward of $500 offered for their apprehension. Albert G. Boyce, a well-known society and club man of Fort Worth, Texas, and Mrs. J. B. (Lena) Sneed, wife of the millionaire canal [sic] contractor of Texas, were arrested in the Royal Alexandra hotel, Winnipeg, yesterday evening. . . . [W]hen crossing the border they claimed that they were man and wife, and it is on this that they are charged with being unlawfully in Canada.[99]

There were, of course, several inaccuracies in this report, the most startling being the obvious confusion of "canal" for "cattle."[100] In Fort Worth, Beal, alert to the advantages that court action could give him, was working to get Al indicted on state charges of rape and abduction. He had just finished testifying before the Seventeenth District grand jury when Dr. Turner informed him that Lena had been detained in Canada.[101] Using the name of John Smith, he purchased a .32 caliber Colt revolver at Anderson's gun store in Fort Worth and departed that evening on the Katy. He reached Winnipeg on Saturday morning, December 30, 1911.[102]

Contrary to the initial newspaper report, Al and Lena were released on bail the day after their first arrest without having been charged.[103] Their counsel in Canada, T. J. Murray, was kept busy over the next few days fielding the various legal ploys generated both in Texas and in Canada.

On December 28, the couple was again arrested. This time, the warrant was based on a telegram from Sheriff W. M. Rea in Fort Worth and stated that Al was charged with grand larceny in Fort Worth.[104] Lena was held without being charged. The larceny charge was predicated on the fact that Lena had left Fort Worth with some jewelry, including diamond rings. When she and Al were first arrested, she had given him two of the rings for safekeeping. These were found in Al's pocket. Beal claimed that the jewelry was his, evidently realizing that Canadian law considered grand larceny an extraditable offense, while abduction was not if the crime occurred outside of Canada.

Murray was able to secure bail for Al and Lena a second time. Meanwhile, the Fort Worth grand jury returned an indictment for abduction against Al on December 30, 1911, the day Beal arrived in Winnipeg. The elder Boyces had made clear their intentions of supporting their son in his attempt to prevent extradition or deportation and in his fight against the charges in Texas: They had testified before the Fort Worth grand jury to defend him. The prestigious Canadian law firm, Campbell, Pitblado, Hoskin & Grundy (which Murray had joined in 1911) was employed to assist Al and, by extension, Lena.

Immediately after Beal's arrival in Winnipeg, he succeeded in getting the lovers arrested for the third time, this time on the charge of entering the country illegally and being "undesirable citizens." This charge was an unbailable offense; through it, Beal could keep the lovers separated and locked up, interview Lena, and pursue punishing her lover. Beal also charged Al with larceny under Canadian law.

Unbeknownst to Beal or the newspapers, Lena had, after her first arrest and release, given all her jewelry to Murray. The larceny charge was flimsy, as Beal well knew; both Al and Lena refused to state where the jewelry was, and although Beal got a warrant to search their quarters at the Immigration Hotel, he failed to find it. Though his preference was to get Al extradited to face legal charges in Texas, he began to focus his efforts instead on deportation—the prescribed penalty for illegal entry. After waiting a few days for necessary papers from the United States government, Beal got Lena deported on January 2, dropping the Canadian larceny charge against Al prior to their departure. Unable to prevent Lena's deportation, Murray succeeded in preventing Al's, arguing that Beal would kill him if Al were forced to cross the line.

As the *Free Press* noted, "[t]he charges against

Boyce are woven around the fact that the woman was feeble-minded . . . that owing to her enfeebled mind Boyce secured a great influence over her and forced her to follow him. It is on these grounds that the charges of abduction, rape and larceny are laid."

Murray, in an effort to have the insanity theory disproved, was reported to have had Lena examined by two "alienists" while she was in Canada. Both declared her sane.[105]

After Beal arrived in Winnipeg, Lena wrote Al several notes from her room in the Immigration Hall. "I feel now like we are lost and oh, Albert, I blame no one but myself and I will never spend another peaceful moment. I loved you too much, darling, I lost sight of what was best for you."[106] She went on to describe her conversation with Beal and the Burns detective who accompanied him:

[T]he Burns man tried to persuade me to go back to Texas with him, said he would go all the way with me to any point I wanted to go + leave Beal here, but I wouldn't consent + he used ever [sic] persuasive power in the world, but of course I didn't believe one word they said—They are tearing my heart out about the children. Beal brought a pr. of G. B.'s [Georgia Beal, their youngest daughter's] shoes that he had in his grip + it almost killed me when I looked at them. He said you would hang as soon as you got to Texas + oh I can't think all he has said. . . . I believe they are going to make trouble about the rings. Beal has tried every way on earth to make me tell where they

*are—He said he would shoot Murrays [sic] head off
if he were in Texas + I am satisfied he will do some
shooting here if everything goes against him. . . . I
believe if they ever take you back they would shut
me up so I couldn't testify for you—Albert I know
[illegible] a divine power to help me or I couldn't have
stood all this.*[107]

Lena left Winnipeg accompanied by Beal,
the Canadian immigration agent, and two
detectives. In Minneapolis, Lena's father, Tom
Snyder, and her brother-in-law, Henry Bowman,
met the couple. Beal instructed Bowman and
Snyder to return Lena to Arlington Heights at
once, then set off again for Winnipeg.[108] There
he made a renewed charge of theft—this time
in the amount of $750—against Al.[109] As soon as
Beal left Minneapolis, Snyder told Bowman "that
he was going to take [Lena] home with him,
regardless of what [Beal] said."[110] Lena returned
with her father to Clayton, New Mexico, where
Snyder and his wife were living with their
daughter, Susan Snyder Pace, and her husband,
John Pace.

The Canadian papers were agog over the
scandal and the hot-blooded Texans in their
midst:

*All three Texans . . . Sneed, Boyce, and John M.
Logan [a Boyce family friend who came to Canada
after Lena's deportation], are described as having one
characteristic in common.*

*All three were quiet in manner and speech, and
courteous to all who met them. There was in all three,*

however, the same apparent disregard for human life, and a low estimate of the heinousness of the crime of manslaughter or murder. Feuds, with accompanying deaths, appeared to have been a common feature of the life of the country, and the shooting of a man as the result of a quarrel seemed to be but little more serious than the shooting of a dumb animal.[111]

In a stem-winding editorial, one Winnipeg paper, underscoring the difference between Canadian and Texan attitudes, excoriated the Canadian officials for their assistance in the "unwarranted persecution" of the "woman . . . to such an extent that she in desperation was forced to return with her husband to the United States."[112] The writer went on:

It is a fine thing, and, oh, what a manly thing!—for a mushy emotionalist to slop over in writing of the "injured husband" and "the erring wife"—but officials of the Canadian government and officials of the police department in Winnipeg are not paid their salaries for the purpose of serving the ends of wife-chasing husbands who attempt to exercise a tyrannical authority by locking their wives up in lunatic asylums in the United States because those wives fail to "love, honor and obey" a male of the human species whose conduct, on his own admission, would make love impossible, honor a confession of depravity, and obedience an encouragement to brute force—Our whole legal machinery is improperly set to work to assist a high-handed husband from Texas in gaining possession of his wife, who seems to have shown mighty good sense in running away from a person who treated her as if she had been a chattel somewhat difficult to control.[113]

On December 31, 1911, the *Star-Telegram* reported an interview with Colonel and Mrs. Boyce, a story that was picked up by the Winnipeg papers. The Boyces, who had been in Fort Worth to testify for Al before the Seventeenth District grand jury, were quoted extensively. The Colonel was reported to have said: "Nobody will believe that my son abducted Lena Sneed. . . . she is as sane as anybody. . . . I know that they sent Mrs. Sneed to the sanitarium to get her away from my son. [There was a letter] addressed it [to] Santa Rosa. It followed [Al] to Dalhart. I have never seen the letter, but my other son in Dalhart [Henry] saw it; Albert showed it to him. . . . she planned the whole thing, and I am going to see that my son's name is cleared of the false charge against him."[114]

Mrs. Boyce spoke thus:

Albert was hypnotized by that woman. She hypnotized her husband, too, or he wouldn't have offered a big reward for her. She has ruined her husband and my son and has broken my heart. . . . Lena Sneed came to see me many times during the last year. . . . She told me she loved my son and that she wanted to be my daughter. She told me that she had asked her husband to let her get a divorce and that she would get a divorce somehow and marry Albert. I told her it would be wrong. . . . I argued with her and did everything I could, and I was so relieved when I heard they had sent her away. . . . I told her what was her trouble, too much money, too much time to waste, and reading too many cheap novels. She was sane as anybody and planned the whole business herself. I am sorry for her in spite of the ruin she has brought upon us. We would rather have followed Albert to his grave than have him do what he has done—he was hypnotized.[115]

As it turned out, the publication of these comments proved to be one of the turning points in the drama. Writing to Henry Boyce from Clayton, Lena described her family as angry with Beal and in favor of a divorce, except for Eula and Henry Bowman, who were keeping the Sneed daughters, and with whom Beal stayed frequently. (Bowman told Lena's oldest sister, Pearl Snyder Perkins, that Lena could not see the children if she were not with Beal, and Lena reported that Bowman had refused to pass along some gifts and notes from Lena for her daughters.)

Unfortunately, "Papa received Mr. Boyce's message apparently suggesting a meeting to discuss the situation and I was so anxious for him to meet [Colonel Boyce] in Dalhart but the very morning the message came, someone sent [Snyder] the Ft. Worth papers with Mrs. Boyce's testimony before the grand jury. The papers were marked and of course I don't know who sent them, but it made him feel pretty bad."

Though Lena stated her father also felt "awful hard at Beal and blame[d] him for all the newspaper notoriety," in the end he proved one of Beal's staunchest allies.[116] Lena, foreshadowing a difficult relationship with her mother-in-law had she and Al succeeded in marrying, complained to him: "Papa is so hurt. . . . how could she do me this way—The Texas papers are full of it—Papa says he don't feel that he can see Mr. Boyce when they have talked about me this way. . . . I begged and pleaded with him to go see him—but he won't do it . . . + oh, darling if your mother hadn't talked so about me—everything would have been alright."[117]

The Canadian authorities, in the meantime, had prevented Beal from "interviewing" Al in Canada. On January 8, Al was released from the Immigration Hall in Winnipeg on condition that he leave the city, go west and "disappear for some ten days or so in order that it might appear that [he] had been deported and returned to Canada later."[118] After Al's disappearance, Beal left Canada again. A telegram from Henry Bowman informed him that Lena was not in the sanitarium. Beal wired Lena's father from Kansas City, asking to meet him in Dallas: "Come with her—will pay expenses, am willing to put her anywhere you say."[119] By this time, the Canadian authorities realized that Murray was holding Lena's jewelry and Al did not expect to be arrested for theft, despite Beal's charge against him.[120]

Lena did not attend the meeting at the Terminal Hotel in Fort Worth on January 11, 1912. Present were Beal, Lena's father, and her sister Pearl.[121] When Tom Snyder returned to Clayton, he was prepared once again to confine Lena to the sanitarium. On January 12, a frantic Lena wired Henry Boyce: "For God's sake protect me. Beal and Henry Bowman are here to put me in an asylum by force."[122]

**Lenora "Lena" Sneed and her daughters
Lenora, left, and Georgia Beal, circa 1910.**
Photo from the author's collection.

2

By January 13, 1912, Lena was back at the Arlington Heights Sanitarium. This time, however, she was not without resources. At Lena's suggestion, Al had hired Pinkertons to follow her from Canada so he would be advised of where she was taken.[123] Earlier in the month, the Colonel had written to her brother-in-law John Pace: "Tell Lena to stand hitched and I'll stand hitched."[124] At some point, probably in Canada, Lena had given power of attorney to the Boyces.[125] They naturally realized that if Lena were judged insane, Al was more likely to be convicted of the abduction charges, and she could not testify for him in a trial. They had anticipated her reconfinement and were eager to get her released. On January 6, Reese Tatum of Tatum & Tatum, the Boyce attorneys in Dalhart, had written to retain an attorney in Fort Worth, expressing the opinion that "[w]hile there is no question that Mrs. Sneed is absolutely sane, and in fact a very smart woman, still they will perhaps use every means they can to have her adjudged insane in order to make it hard on Boyce."[126] Henry Boyce later explained that he did not want "to see Lena shot full of dope and taken before a county judge and declared insane and Al railroaded to the pen."[127]

The Colonel's "stand hitched" letter was a central document in Beal's murder trials. The defense claimed it indicated the Colonel's involvement in a conspiracy to steal Lena. It seems more likely, given Colonel and Mrs. Boyce's evident reluctance to involve themselves prior to Beal's legal actions against Al, that the Colonel was attempting to make certain that, if he put his money and reputation on the line to defend his son and his son's love affair, his son's paramour was not going to get a case of cold feet.

On January 13, the day Lena was once again confined to the sanitarium, Colonel Boyce was also in Fort Worth. There, he succeeded in getting the state abduction and rape charges against Al dropped. That evening, Beal, Henry Bowman, and U.S. District Attorney Will Atwell walked into the Metropolitan Hotel in Fort Worth to find the Colonel, ensconced in one of the lobby's comfortable chairs, chatting with an acquaintance.

Will Atwell was married to one of Lena's cousins. In what would clearly be considered a conflict of interest by today's standards, Atwell had agreed to serve as Beal's personal attorney in November 1911 and then, acting in his official capacity, had ordered a watch on the Boyces' mail in an attempt to locate the lovers. He later spearheaded the effort to have Al charged with violations of the federal white slavery law.[128] Now, he spoke briefly to the Colonel, while Beal and Bowman waited outside. According to Atwell, the Colonel told him he was planning to leave the hotel shortly and take the train back to Amarillo that night. He requested time to present his witnesses before Atwell proceeded with the federal charges. Over supper at Joseph's, a restaurant not far from the hotel, Atwell described the conversation to Beal and Bowman: Boyce, he said, had stated he could prove in half an hour what "kind of a woman Mrs. Sneed was."[129]

Aware that his wife had given power of attorney to his enemies; having read the "stand hitched" letter, which Tom Snyder had showed him on the train; knowing that the state charges against Al had been dismissed and that his wife was likely to have an attorney at her disposal for a habeas corpus hearing; and believing that the Colonel had made incendiary remarks about Lena, Beal returned to the hotel after supper. He claimed later he wanted to use the toilet (although such facilities were available at the restaurant) and was surprised that the Colonel was still in the lobby and not on his way to the train station. Drawing the gun he had purchased at Anderson's several weeks earlier from the pocket of his overcoat, Beal fired on the old man as he sat in his chair.[130] Boyce rose and staggered as Beal continued to fire. Five or six shots rang out; the startled hotel guests dove for cover. The

Colonel fell. Beal rushed out through the lobby's revolving doors. An ambulance was quickly summoned, but the Colonel died on the way to the hospital.[131]

In Regina, Canada, Al sat writing a letter to Lena: *I was interrupted here by the following telegram being brought to me: 'Associated Press dispatch states Sneed shot and killed Albert's father tonight. Am assured report reliable. On no account allow Albert return to Texas. This probably means opening feud. Answer. T. J. Murray.' I will go to Winnipeg tomorrow. . . . I may return at once to Texas. I don't know. It will be my pleasure and duty to avenge him. Pa was the best of fathers and best and noblest of men and to think of his being killed in his old age by this kind of a brute is awful. I can't write more. I love you with all the strength I possess and will to my death.*[132]

Lena did not learn of the murder until she was brought from the sanitarium to testify before the grand jury. She wrote to Al:

Mr. Boyce had been dead three days before I knew anything about it—you know Beal had shut me up again at Arlington Heights—+ killed your dear father at the Metropolitan about one hour afterwards—this was on Sat. and I was summonded [sic] before the Grand Jury Tues. aft [January 16, 1912] + didn't know anything about it until I left the Grand Jury room—I had my trial for my sanity on Friday [January 19, 1912], + was released from the Sanitarium— Darling it was horrible—they asked the vilest most horrible questions and I had to answer them. It was so horrible all of it was not allowed to be published in the newspapers.[133]

Murray was not the only one convinced that a feud had begun. The Boyces believed it would be far easier to get a conviction against Beal if Al remained in Canada. Hoping to forestall a wholesale shooting war, and to end, once and for all, his relationship with Lena, the family urged him to stay put.[134] In Fort Worth, two camps were established. The Sneed camp—Beal's father and two of Beal's uncles, as well as his brothers, Joe and Marvin—took rooms at the Siebold Hotel. The Boyce camp—Al's brothers Will, Henry, and Lynn, and their friends—stayed at the Westbrook. Both sides consulted night and day with their attorneys. Any move made by the lawyers on one side was immediately countered by lawyers on the other. Each contingent had a strong following of "rich and powerful West Texans. The two hotels resemble political conventions. Almost every minute messages are brought in assuring support and promising financial aid. Hundreds of western cattlemen, capitalists and bankers have taken sides."[135]

As her letter indicates, Lena had acquired her own counsel and succeeded in being released from the sanitarium on a writ of habeas corpus. On the day of her hearing, Beal's attorneys, McLean, Scott & McLean, filed an intervention plea claiming that for her own good she "should not be turned loose in the world at this time."[136] The courtroom was full of prominent and expensive lawyers. Lena was represented by state Senator Offa Shivers "O.S." Lattimore. State senator W.A. Hanger represented the Boyces, who had hired him to assist in Beal's prosecution.[137] Dr. Wilmer Allison, testifying about Lena's mental state, was represented by a former Texas attorney general and a former county judge. D.A. Will Atwell was also in court and was quoted as saying he believed "Mrs. Sneed wished to withdraw the application and 'go with her family.'"[138] Beal's own habeas corpus hearing was delayed so that Lena's case could be heard, though Beal was in the courtroom and there saw Lena for the first time since he had shot the Colonel.

"Of course, the court will understand that a person can't be locked up for moral insanity in Texas," Senator Lattimore declared, and proceeded to subject Dr. Allison to a searing cross-examination:

"You say you treated her—how did you treat her?"

"That is hard to say."

"Did you treat her this morning or yesterday?"

"I could hardly say without looking it up . . ."

"What medicine did you give? . . ."

"Calomel, for one thing, and a tonic . . ."

"Isn't she your highest-priced patient . . . paying $65 while the regular price is $35?"

"The rate varies according to the amount of attention a patient demands and the amount of care necessary."

In response to a rapid fire of questions, Dr.

Allison said Mrs. Sneed caused a great deal of trouble by often asking to talk to him and by constantly wanting to do something or go somewhere.

"Didn't you go to her room last Tuesday night and try for two hours to find out what she had testified before the grand jury, relative to your institution? . . ."

"No . . ."

"Didn't you ask her what the grand jury had asked about the sanitarium?"

"I don't think so . . ."

"Do you think she was of unsound mind? . . ."

"I think she was in a condition of moral insanity . . ."

"What do you mean? . . ."

"That is hard to explain . . ."

"I think so too, but you are an expert . . ."

"I mean a person that has lost their moral sense to a certain extent . . ."

"Is calomel a remedy for moral insanity?"

"That was part of the treatment."[139]

Judge Tom Simmons of the Sixty-seventh District Court ordered three physicians to examine Lena. All declared her sane. According to the *Fort Worth Star-Telegram*, "She remained self-possessed . . . during the frank discussion of her mental condition . . . [in] her statement she made no effort to win sympathy for herself or condone her elopement and made no statements in regard to it."[140]

Lena's voice was the only sound in the

courtroom as she spoke. She claimed that she was put into the sanitarium by force, carried away, and given a hypodermic of apomorphia that rendered her unconscious; that during her first stay, she was allowed only one bath and had been kept for a time in only her nightgown and kimona[sic]. She said she was locked in a hall with insane people. At the conclusion of her evidence, Judge Simmons ordered her liberty: "After hearing this testimony, I could not conclude there was a semblance of insanity developed here in this case, and I am clearly of the opinion that the applicant ought to be discharged, and I will discharge her."[141]

At some point prior to her next letter to Al, written February 2, 1912, Lena saw her daughters:

[I]t would have made your heart ache to have seen how they clung to me and cried when I had to leave them, + Beal told Billie Steele [an old friend, whose sister had married one of Lena's brothers] they wouldn't have a thing to do with him when he went over there. . . . [The Bowmans] told me unless I would say I thought Beal was justified in what he did, they didn't want me to stay there—so of course I left—+ I never had a place in the world to go nor any money so I phoned Pearl + she came + drew on you at Dalhart.[142]

The issue of money was always present for Lena. Al made it clear to her that "what I have is yours and I want you to feel as free to use it as I do myself." Drawing checks from Al's account in the bank in Dalhart, however, meant making her monetary needs clear to Henry Boyce, the cashier at the bank. She was, by this time, uncertain how Henry felt about her[143] and sure that Mrs. Boyce detested her. She was also doubtless uncomfortable with the idea that any of the Boyces might know how much money she was taking from Al. The subject of money runs through her letters like a small tributary of the mighty river of passion, but clearly it was of the utmost practical importance. Al seems to have been unfailingly generous with her, at least judging from comments in her letters thanking him for unsolicited funds[144] or telling him, in response to his apparent question, that she did not need more.[145] When the draft on the Dalhart bank was returned, Lena urged Al to sell his stock in the family bank.[146] Later, she reconsidered, at least to the extent of writing:

Darling I wrote and asked you to sell your bank stock—but don't do it unless you want to for your people would no doubt blame me—I haven't drawn on you for any money darling as I have over two hundred dollars. . . . I feel just as free to what you have dear as if it were mine—you are so sweet and generous—and we must both be saving . . .[147]

After her release from the sanitarium, a regular correspondence was established between the lovers, especially while Lena stayed with her sister Pearl at the Perkins' house in Lake Charles, Louisiana.[148] Pearl, alone among Lena's family members, steadfastly supported her relationship with Al.

The trial for the murder of Colonel Boyce began
after Beal had been freed on $35,000 bail.[149] Both
a motion for continuance and a motion to move
the trial from the court of Judge James R. "J.W."
Swayne had been denied.[150] Judge Swayne had
begun his career as a city attorney determined
to clean up Hell's Half Acre, Fort Worth's
notorious vice district. He had experienced
a notable lack of success in prosecuting
violations of city gambling laws, because the
juries hearing the cases were entirely unwilling
to convict men used to paying a small fine for
their indiscretions and returning immediately
to work. Nonetheless, as city attorney, Swayne
had demonstrated a dogged regard for law and
order.[151] It was perhaps this quality that made
Beal's attorneys so eager to get the case before
another judge. Despite their efforts, however,
jury selection began in Swayne's courtroom in
the Seventeenth District on January 31, 1912.[152]

The jury was selected slowly, at least by
the standards of the day. Each prospective
juror was asked if he believed in a man's right
to protect fully his home and household. By
February 4, twelve jurors had been selected. In
the innocent custom of bygone times, a photo
of the group was published, each was named in
the newspaper, and their occupations, marital
status and addresses were listed. They ranged in
age from twenty-three to forty-four. All but one
were married, all but one were southern born

(and that one had moved south at the age of ten months). Needless to say, all were males. Judge Swayne, anticipating a relatively lengthy trial, again, by the standards of the day, announced that he would try to arrange for baths.[153]

The trial itself revolved around several issues. The stale claimed that Beal, without reason, had killed the unarmed and defenseless Colonel in cold blood. The defense contended that from the first time the Boyces had aided and abetted Al in eloping with Lena, they had decided to steal her for their own family. The Colonel had been instrumental in the plot. The defense also contended that the Colonel had said insulting things about Lena—or at least that Beal had been told the Colonel had said insulting things—and that he had insulted Beal when he saw him in the Metropolitan lobby the night of the killing, though the last seems highly doubtful.[154] The defense tactic was essentially the old ploy of putting the victim on trial by demonizing the Boyces, particularly the males. Writing to Al on February 2, 1912, Lena remarked, "Judge Swayne + public opinion is against Beal."[155] By the trial's end, however, public opinion had apparently changed.[156]

Through the course of the trial, a picture emerged of the relationships among the three families prior to October 1911; of their gradual recognition of the nature of the relationship between Lena and Al; and of the efforts to control or thwart it made by the Boyces, Tom Snyder

Sr., and Beal's older brother, Joe. Despite the defense's contentions, it is difficult to conclude that the Boyces were up to much of anything until after Beal charged Al with abduction and larceny. The most plausible scenario is that the Boyces, the parents in particular, deplored the relationship. After Al was charged, however, they became involved because they did not want their son to go to prison and did not think the charges were justified. As a result of that decision, and probably also because of things Al may have written about Lena and her marriage to his family from Canada,[157] and because, as everyone who knew him seemed to agree, once "he set his head in a certain way he was hard to control . . . [and] [t]hey could do nothing with him,"[158] the Boyces decided they had to help Lena. Within a few days of her return from Canada, the Colonel had sent the "stand hitched" letter. Naturally, this document was central to the defense.

Colonel Boyce was, by all accounts, a determined man with a strong personality. He had been hired by the Farwells, the Chicago-based owners of the XIT, in part to clean the ranch up and rid it of the gamblers, rustlers, and drunks who infested it.[159] This he did, and throughout his tenure maintained a rigorous order. Told once by the foreman at the Spring Lake Division that a discharged cowboy refused to leave, Boyce appeared at breakfast with a six-shooter in his lap. When the cowboy showed up for his coffee and biscuits, Boyce uttered the immortal

Western line: "This ranch is not big enough for both of us." It was not, and the Colonel was not the one to leave.[160] That the Colonel may have expressed himself in forceful terms not always flattering to Beal or Lena, or to Al for that matter, seems more than likely. His comments about Lena, in particular, were verified by a number of disinterested witnesses.[161]

On the other hand, one of the main defense witnesses was W.H. Fuqua, a cattle broker, neighbor of the Boyces and the Sneeds, and president of the First National Bank of Amarillo. There was bad blood between Fuqua and Colonel Boyce over the attempt in 1901 by minor stockholders to place the XIT in receivership. Fuqua was involved in this move, which Boyce resisted when receivers appeared at ranch headquarters in Channing. Leaning his Winchester against the door, Boyce told the receivers that he did not propose to turn anything over to them and that he would resist force with force.[162]

Judging from a letter Beal sent to him on November 23, 1911, Fuqua was not only Beal's banker and sometimes-partner in cattle broker deals, but a close friend as well.

I want to thank you from the bottom of my heart for what you have done for me. I have thought and thought and tried to think and I don't see why God wants me to suffer and suffer and yet live. . . . You know I love the little children and would gladly give my life for them. But she loved them more than I, and I

*will always know that had she been herself she would
have stood to be burned and tortured to death before
she would have heaped this ignominy and disgrace on
their little lives. . . . [S]he would sympathize with me
and help me as no one else could, instead of killing
me by degrees. . . . I am sure it will be only a matter
of time until she will be the most miserable of human
beings and probably become more insane. Or should
she recover her mind by some act of Providence she
would be just as miserable and probably destroy
herself. . . . You may think this is a crazy letter, and it
may be, but at the same time I feel that you will come
nearer understanding the motive which prompted it
than anyone else, and that is the reason I have written
it.*[163]

Beal visited Amarillo two or three times in
December 1911. Each time, he saw Fuqua. "Mr.
Fuqua told him that Capt. Boyce was doing a lot
of talking around. He said Boyce was making
vile, dirty talk all over town and Fuqua wouldn't
humiliate him by repeating it."[164] With the
courtroom cleared of the many women who
attended the trial, Fuqua testified as to precisely
what these comments were, though the papers
refused to print them. In one instance, Fuqua
testified, the Colonel was chatting with a group of
men in L.O. Thompson's drugstore in Amarillo.
Someone asked what it was about Lena that
made one man willing to spend twenty thousand
to steal her and another man willing to spend
twenty thousand to get her back. Evidently,
the Colonel's theory was a crude one.[165] Fuqua

informed Beal of the nature, if not the exact wording, of these remarks, a move that, under the circumstances, was hardly calculated to cool things off.

Tom Snyder testified with real fury about Colonel Boyce's part in the affair, claiming that the Colonel had "betrayed [their] friendship of fifty years and had sacrificed the Sneed and Snyder families to save his 'drunken son.'"[166] Joe Sneed Sr. by contrast, was more restrained, saying that he and Colonel Boyce agreed that Lena and Al were equally culpable and that Beal should divorce her. They differed only, and predictably, over whether Beal should pay alimony.[167]

In some ways, the story as it emerged in the trial is about the rebellion of three children against their close-knit fathers. Lena rebelled not only against Beal, but also ultimately against her father, who infuriated her by taking Beal's part.[168] Beal rebelled against his father, who wanted him to give Lena up, a fact that is reflected in the relative "coolness" of J.T. Sneed Sr.'s testimony, compared to Tom Snyder's. And Al, of course, the "uncontrollable," rebelled against what must surely have been his father's original desire that he abandon his infatuation. In this sense, the Colonel's murder is not as extraneous as it may at first appear. The three fathers—Tom Snyder, Joe Sneed Sr., and Colonel A.G. Boyce— represented a generation of powerful men who had heretofore controlled their worlds effectively and completely. Their closeness can be gauged

**Boyce family members in the parlor of
the Channing, Texas, home. Circa 1898.
From left, Albert G. Boyce Jr., Lynn Boyce,
Mrs. Annie Boyce, Bessie Boyce, and
Albert G. Boyce Sr.**
Photo courtesy of the XIT Museum, Dalhart, Texas

not only through their testimony, but in the ways that other participants refer to them. Henry Boyce addressed Tom Snyder as "Uncle Tom." When Will Atwell talked with Colonel Boyce an hour or so before his death, he hailed him as "Uncle Al." The formulation makes the men brothers, and viewed from this perspective, the drama becomes not only erotic, but also familial: A story of the shattering of paternal power and the severance of fraternal ties.

Mrs. Boyce was put on the stand and testified about the beginning of the affair.

"The first act I didn't approve of . . . was when he took her to the opera house in the fall of 1910. . . . I told him, 'This is not New York City. This is not four hundred society. I do not think Beal Sneed would like this. This is imprudent."

After that, she testified, Al was gone much of the time, and she saw nothing to cause her "fresh uneasiness," until the summer of 1911 when Al began to visit Lena in the morning and afternoon. On July 22, 1911—an election day— Lena called at the Boyce home while Colonel Boyce was out campaigning for Cone Johnson (ironically, now a defense lawyer).[169]

The defense was able repeatedly to suppress evidence about what Lena said to Mrs. Boyce and even about what Mrs. Boyce said. Mary Hamilton, a cousin of Mrs. Boyce who lived at the Boyce home, was in the room when Lena and Mrs. Boyce had their discussion. Lena apparently expressed her love for Al, according to Hamilton's testimony, and said she wanted a divorce from Beal. Over the objections of the defense, Hamilton testified that Mrs. Boyce said: "'Oh, Lena, I never thought it would come to this. I knew you were imprudent, but I never thought of such a thing as this. What would Beal think of this?'" She then talked to Lena about her children.[170]

Mrs. Boyce, despite grief and ill health, proved an estimable witness. "[S]he belongs to the pioneer type of American womanhood who could stand by the side of the fighters and load muskets while she saw her loved ones being shot down around her. No more magnificent evidence of the courage of the freeborn American woman [has] ever been given in this state," wrote a clearly impressed Kitty Barry, who provided "color" and the "distaff" perspective for the *Star-Telegram*.[171]

Mrs. Boyce testified that she did not know Lena was to be "put where there were insane people."[172] If Lena "had been the least bit insane when this thing first started . . . she would be a raving maniac by now. . . . Had I known that [Lena] was going to be put in an asylum . . . I would have objected."[173] Asked point blank if Lena was insane, Mrs. Boyce snapped, "No, she wasn't. She was nervous; Al was nervous; everybody was nervous; there ought to have been more people nervous."[174]

When cross-examined by defense counsel W.P. "Wild Bill" McLean Jr. about why she was so concerned that Lena might be sent to a sanitarium, she replied, "I wouldn't have put a child of mine in a place where there were crazy people."

"You wouldn't have put Albert there?"

"No, sir."

"Don't you think a man running over and disgracing his mother and father and stealing another man's wife and killing that man's little children—don't you think such a man a fit subject for the asylum or penitentiary?"[175]

At that point, Lynn Boyce ("tall, taciturn and Western," according to Kitty Barry[176]), whose courtroom habit throughout the trial was to whittle, lunged at McLean. Lynn was fined and sent to jail for an hour, and Mrs. Boyce never answered the question. Reportedly, she remained so calm she sent smelling salts to her son.[177] At this distance in time, her testimony has the ring of truth in its portrayal of a family trying to deal with a messy situation in which neither of the primary players could be controlled.

There were some notable absences on the witness list, including that of Beal's brother, Joe Sneed Jr. But most notable of all was the absence of Lena, an absence that made it possible for the defense to suppress testimony that quoted her because her statements could not be used against her husband. The defense had subpoenaed her, then declined to call her to the stand. "There is not a man in the defense of this case but [who] honestly believes that the woman was insane and [is] insane now," was Bill McLean Jr.'s explanation of the defense decision.[178] In fact, as her letters reveal, Lena refused to testify for Beal:

Oh my boy you will never know or understand the pleadings + persuasion I have withstood. Beal's lawyers—+ everyone have offered every inducement to try + make me testify for him. They pleaded for the sake of the children—+ oh, Albert it was awful. They said I could clear him if I would just testify that your father had influenced me + knew where we were, + that I didn't realize what I had done. I told them I knew nothing to tell + if I did I wouldn't tell it. That I wouldn't tell a lie to save him—+ that if I was going to tell a lie to save him I wouldn't lie on the dead—+ when they saw it was useless, you see what McLean has had to say about no court believing my testimony on account of me being insane.[179]

So many years after the murders, one wonders: Did Beal abuse Lena? In part, the answer to this question depends on how one defines the term; the present definition is far more commodious than the meaning assigned in 1912. Al seems to have thought so. There was testimony to the effect that after Lena told Beal she wanted a divorce, she tried to prevent him from using the phone to wire her father, and he fought her with sufficient force to leave bruises on her arm and neck.[180] Mrs. Boyce described her as "terribly bruised,"[181] but others, including her father and sister, saw her injuries as minor.[182] Beal himself testified that he picked her up and "laid" her on the bed[183] prior to attempting to kill her. This was probably a more violent act than Beal made it sound and certainly the effort to kill her was hardly pacific. By the standards of our time, the unjustified commitment to the sanitarium is clearly abusive—an opinion which Judge Simmons and Mrs. Boyce shared. But the defense and others saw it as charitable in comparison to the alternatives of death or divorce. Lena's own father thought Beal ought to whip her and went on to say that he himself was tempted to "put her over his knee."[184] The *Manitoba Free Press* claimed that Lena "bore testimony to [Beal's] selfishness, his preoccupation, his arrogance and his jealousy . . . [and] some of those who had to do with [him] in Winnipeg [have] it that he was a person of violent and malignant temper."[185] It is hard to believe, however, that if Beal had been as possessive as Lena supposedly claimed (at least prior to her revelation) that he would have remained oblivious to, or tacitly accepted, a relationship about which everyone else in the neighborhood must have been aware.

Lena's letters to Al were, predictably, full of disparaging comments about Beal. It is therefore notable that she did not claim that he beat her or had ever done so. She was, on the other hand, at times afraid that he would kill her.[186] In one of her notes to Al in Canada, she wrote, "[Beal] is nothing but a demon— + now he will be meaner to me than ever."[187] Somehow the word "mean" does not carry the weight one expects to describe sustained abusive behavior. In the only instance in which Lena alludes to the marriage prior to her affair, she writes, "I did try so hard to be a good wife to him + to please him—but it was his iron will—+ contemptible dirty ways that he tries to hide that killed all my feeling over four years ago I ever had for him."[188]

The term "iron will" certainly seems to apply to this man, both in the view of him provided by Lena's letters,[189] obviously biased though they are, and in the impression created by his own letters written on matters of business in the years following the trials.[190] Indeed, his insistence on keeping a wife who had indicated in every possible way that she did not want to stay married to him, evidence a will for which steel or some other even harder substance may be a more appropriate metaphor. Judging by his testimony, by the letter to Fuqua, and even by his photographs, Beal seems to have possessed, in addition to an implacable will, a kind of belligerent self-pity. Examples abound in our own time of the ways in which this combination—particularly when massaged, as it was by Beal's defense attorneys, into a martyr theme—can serve to provoke public sympathy, however unattractive it may be in private life. Clearly the craftiest of the three principals, Beal seems to have understood exactly what behavior might be viewed as abusive and what could be made to appear as the acts of a concerned husband, regardless of their true motivations. Confining Lena to a sanitarium, intercepting mail from her lover, limiting her access to her children as long as she refused to reconcile with him—all these were acts he could defend. By the standards of his time, at least in the eyes of many, these were not instances of abuse, particularly under the circumstances and given his intentions as the defense characterized them.

Henry Boyce had served as Al's financial advisor and family contact after the elopement, a fact he freely admitted, while denying his father was in any way involved.[191] The defense brought out telephone logs listing each call made from one Boyce to another, from Dalhart to Amarillo and back again, in an attempt to show that all the Boyces not only knew where Al and Lena were but aided them in their entire journey. In addition, they produced a number of telegrams sent by Henry to Al, Al to Henry, Lena to Henry, Henry to his father, etc.[192] Although Henry did inform his parents when Al and Lena got to Omaha, and again when they reached Winnipeg, Mrs. Boyce claimed they believed the couple would be moving on.[193] The Colonel apparently said publicly several times he thought Al was in South America, although some of those occasions more or less coincided with times when he got news of Al's actual whereabouts.[194] Nevertheless, there seems to have been no sustained contact between the Boyce parents and Al. Both Henry and William, the eldest son and an able attorney, must certainly have realized, if none of the other Boyces did, that it was best to keep things on a "need to know" basis. All the mail going to 1104 Polk Street was being opened in an effort to locate the lovers.[195] Though the defense certainly interpreted it differently, the telegram Henry sent to Canada in late December 1911—reporting the abduction charges and informing Al that "Beal's latest move puts Pa in the game"[196]—implies that the Colonel had not been "in the game" before, but was now responding to Beal's legal maneuvers against Al. In retrospect, the case against the Colonel seems based less on hard facts than on his sometimes-overbearing personality and on his unfortunate tendency to talk too much to the wrong people.

Beal himself proved a stellar witness. "The defendant is making a great witness, his lawyers say, and the same sentiment is expressed by those who heard him," reported the *Star-Telegram* on February 14, 1912. On the stand on Valentine's Day for six hours and fifteen minutes, Beal gave his version of the events that led to the killing of the Colonel. He emphasized his happiness with his home life until his wife informed him that she wanted a divorce, and his desire to help her regain her health and sanity. Georgia Beal's shoe, which he had brought to show Lena in Winnipeg, and which had so wrung her heart, had been transformed into a shoe she had tied around her neck and worn there since her elopement, a detail that received much play in the *Star-Telegram*.[197] "'And my wife had one of Georgia Beal's baby shoes tied round her neck and she took it out and crushed it in her arms and cried over it,'" began Kitty Barry's account of Beal's testimony.[198] Barry went on to remark that she noticed tears in the eyes of one of the jurors as Beal spoke. "Many other men," she reported, "took out their handkerchiefs, too, and wiped their eyes and looked downward with flushed faces," as Beal recounted the story of his dreary Christmas with his daughters at the Bowman house in 1911, when Lenora begged him to bring her mother back. The vision of the happy home despoiled by the hard-drinking Al Boyce, whose family supported him in his lechery, and of the suffering husband and children, was evidently immensely effective with the family men on the jury. [199] Beal made certain his two girls were in court at least some of the time, a practice which Lena deplored,[200] but which clearly won Beal sympathy from the jury and at least tacit approval from Kitty Barry, whose sympathetic description of the two girls with their father never raises the issue of the appropriateness of their presence.[201]

Public interest in the trial's closing arguments was high. On a rainy February 22 in Fort Worth, well-dressed matrons packed the courthouse. One woman stabbed another with a hatpin to secure a seat.[202]

Cone Johnson's summation went on for over four hours; The audience was spellbound, and jurymen cried.[203] Some excerpts from the speech follow:

This case . . . must be considered . . . solely and alone from the standpoint of the defendant. . . .

[T]he law says the thing for us to do is to get in his shoes and see how he was surrounded and how he looked at it. . . .

If a man should spit in my face and denounce me and I kill him on the spot, then I could be found guilty of no higher degree than manslaughter. But if I went away and reflected and came back and killed him, the degree would be higher.

But there is another phase which the law of Texas and Southern chivalry says shall not be limited by time. If a man strikes an insult to a female relative, the barb may be carried for years in the breast and the insulter then killed at the first opportunity. That is the law in the South when a man heaps an insult on our womenfolks.

Beal Sneed is the only man I have ever heard of or read of since the days of Christ that has stood by his wife through all circumstances. There was a time when it was said an eye for an eye . . . but there came another time when a man stood by the Sea of Galilee and said, 'Go and sin no more' and changed the old law which said if a woman is taken, let her be stoned.'

Capt. Boyce had written [to the Canadian authorities, attempting to persuade them to let Al remain as a citizen] that Al Boyce was a good citizen, but the woman was as 'mean as the devil.'

The miserable, contemptible doctrine that a man who debauches a woman, even another man's wife, will make a good citizen, but the woman is as mean as the devil and must be cast out is what is undermining American civilization and spreading the poison. . . .

Why, they talked about the taking of this man's

wife like she was a cow they were squabbling over. Boyce writing, 'Lena, you stand hitched and I'll stand hitched to the end.' They got that idea just like it was a cow transaction. . . .

Did you notice those two little children, gentlemen? They are parties to this case. You can't render a verdict that won't reach them. Send this man to the penitentiary and Beal Sneed is robbed of all right to control those little children. This other crowd here already, through Al Boyce, destroyed these little children's mother and now they are asking this jury to make a felon of their father. . . . We have had sorrow enough. There's the home of Beal Sneed at Amarillo gone forever. Its inhabitants scattered; the father here standing trial for his life. . . . The Boyces ought to be satisfied. The Sneeds ought to feel that there's been enough calamity. Beal Sneed will go somewhere with his little children and begin life over again, as he said he would do at first.[204]

Within the first ten minutes of deliberations, the jury hung seven to five in favor of acquittal. Despite Judge Swayne's adamant insistence that it continue to deliberate and render a verdict, the vote never changed, and the jury never budged. On February 29, 1912, after several days of battling with the jurymen, Judge Swayne at last declared a mistrial.[205]

On March 3, the *Star-Telegram* reported that Wilmer and Bruce Allison had been indicted for restraining a woman named Irene George of her liberty. The circumstances were very like those about which Lena had testified in her habeas hearing. George contended she had been confined in her room, deprived of her clothing, and not allowed to see her children.[206] In a related court action, Mrs. George was represented by Lena's counsel, O.S. Lattimore, who won George's acquittal on charges of lunacy despite the fact that her father contended that "his daughter's mental condition was aggravated by reading the accounts of the Sneed trial."[207]

Judge Swayne, in admonishing the Sneed jury about its failure to deliver a verdict, had commented that "[t]his case has attracted the widest attention of any case ever tried in Texas, and every feature has been published all over the world. The world knows what the testimony is, and it has put Texas on trial."[208]

The "Texan-ness" of the case was, of course, a feature that many had noted—from the titillated Canadian newspapers to Beal's unabashed apologist, Cone Johnson. The defense made no bones about choosing married jurymen who hailed from states south of the Mason-Dixon line and who had lived in Texas for some time. Johnson's mixture of sentimentality, fierceness, emphasis on honor, and ritualized protectiveness toward women was Texan and Southern in the highest degree. As a means of "framing" the case, the speech was clearly persuasive to at least seven of the jury members. For the public, the case was profoundly disturbing. That disturbance is indicated not only by the huge interest in the story and the packed courtroom throughout the trial, but also by the almost preternatural level of violence and illness that attended it. The Irene George case is a small example of a sort of ripple effect that the story seemed to have on those around it, whether in the ways that George's father alleged, or in her own recognition that she might have recourse to being locked up against her will.

A brief list of some of the "peripheral" deaths related to or associated with the trial further illuminates this point. First among these was the death of E.C. Throckmorton, a Boyce family friend who was chatting with the Colonel at the time Beal shot him. As a principal witness, Throckmorton had testified before the grand jury. Then, on January 27, he was mysteriously taken ill and never recovered. The circumstances seemed suspicious and, given the nature of his testimony—that Beal stood over the Colonel's prostrate form saying, "Now you're out of it"[209]—auspicious for the defense. Nevertheless, plans for an autopsy were abandoned after it was discovered that Throckmorton's family had already had him embalmed. The general conclusion was that Throckmorton died of alcohol poisoning.[210]

Then on February 14, 1912, the same day that Beal took the stand, a Frank Kirklen killed a Walter Eugene Slayton over the latter's plans to marry Kirklen's ex-wife. That killing occurred at Ninth and Main, the intersection the Metropolitan Hotel occupied. Next, on February

19, 1912, Ben U. Bell—a detective associated with the defense—shot S.S. Morris to death in a quarrel over disparaging remarks Morris made about Lena on a crowded streetcar.[211]

The *Star-Telegram* noted the "illness hoodoo" that haunted the trial: Mrs. Boyce, Cone Johnson, Judge Swayne, and various jurors and attorneys had all been sick at one time or another.[212] One cannot, of course, link such illnesses and peripheral deaths in any inarguable way to the facts of the story. Yet, taken together, they leave the impression of a kind of collective trouble in the Zeitgeist.

By far the most sensational of this series of incidents, however, and the one that most directly affected Beal, occurred six days after Judge Swayne dismissed the jury. Beal's father, J.T. Sneed Sr., was shot to death on March 6, 1912, while leaving the post office in Georgetown. His killer was R.O. Hillard, a tenant farmer who then killed himself. A note to his wife said Hillard blamed Sneed, a former landlord, for his insanity.[213] Naturally, there was a frenzy of initial speculation that the Boyces were behind the death, but this was not the case. Lena, in Dallas at the time of the killing, reported seeing "men and women fight on the streets for the papers" that covered the story.[214] As Lena also noted in a letter to Al, the death was helpful to Beal, at least in the financial sense, because he inherited a seventh of his father's estate, the rest being divided among his siblings, his stepmother, and her two children.[215]

Unraveling the mysteries of the Zeitgeist is, of course, endlessly fascinating and eternally speculative in nature. Women, as well as men, were deeply interested by the trial. Much of the interest on the part of both sexes was naturally because of the case's sensational nature. The gender-based conventions in the courtroom clearly measure the distance between 1912 and our own time: Because of the women in court, smoking—in which most of the men, at least judging from Kitty Barry's account, would have indulged—was banned.[216] Barry also believed that the female presence had a marked effect on the witnesses: "Hardly a witness is called who does not show in some way during the progress of his testimony the deterring effect of the proximity of the feminine sex."[217] While at the trial's beginning, men chivalrously offered their seats to women, by the end this was no longer so frequent. Judge Swayne politely requested that the women in the front rows remove their large, fashionable hats so that people in the back of the courtroom could see. When scarcely a woman complied, he was forced to turn his request into an order. If the testimony became particularly salacious, as in the case of W.H. Fuqua's account of the Colonel's remarks, women were barred from the courtroom, presumably including Kitty Barry.

Barry commented on the crowds of women attending the trial: *The women present day after day are practically the same ones, and the majority of them do not belong to that rapidly growing class of American women who are proudly interested in all the phases of existence common to humanity. They do not appear to be women who come there for instruction in the inside working of the judiciary system, because the expressions for the most part on their faces are frankly curious and not studiously analytical.*

This facial expression of curiosity intensifies when the evidence tends in any way toward involving personal issues and personal characteristics of the defendant. The fundamental feminine view is essentially personal. Only the woman student of books or of people and conditions can in any appreciable degree ally her attitude with the impersonal. The women at the Sneed trial do not seem to be able to do this in a successful degree. . . . During the routine of the examinations, they are looking at the toes of their shoes or fumbling with their dress accessories or whispering very quietly to each other.

Although one doubts that most of the men attending the trial were primarily interested in its analytic aspects, Barry was nothing if not confident of her ability to see what others might miss. On the same day that she voiced her opinion of the women at the trial, she tracked Lena down at the Worth Hotel. Citing Lena's "slight uncertainty of motion and speech, scarcely noticeable, [and] unmeaning gestures with hands and shoulder," Barry concluded that there was "an almost indefinable impression of the lack of absolute and sure control. . . .

The individual unused to observation analysis, however," she went on, "would hardly notice these character indications."[218]

"The lack of absolute and sure control." However quaint or humorous one might find Barry's comments, the issue of control went to the heart of the case. In the accounts of Beal's first trial, more heavily covered by the newspapers than either of the subsequent two, one gets a view of public opinion crystallizing. By the time of his final trial, almost exactly a year later, the public was not interested in revisiting its interpretation of the story, at least so one gathers from both the frank prejudice in Beal's favor expressed by prospective jurymen and a certain level of perfunctoriness in the newspaper coverage. The job of both defense and prosecution in any trial, of course, is to tell a story that the jury will buy. The successful story, in a case of this magnitude, may reveal much more about the fears, prejudices, and hopes of the jury and the public than it does about the nature of the real people who figure as the story's main characters.

As has been discussed, the "stories" in the Fort Worth trial pitted a view of Beal's motives against a view of the Colonel's. In terms of the disturbance the case induced, however, one comes to believe that it was the interpretation of Lena's motives that lay at the trial's heart. Silent as she was in the public record, she became in court almost a paper doll figure that the defense and prosecution might dress as they chose.

The fundamental strategy of the defense was to wall off the objectionable or troubling portion of her behavior and call it the result of her insanity. This formulation robbed her of the will or rationality to make any defensible decision other than to remain with Beal and her children. If she were sane, she would choose to give Al up and return to family life with Beal; the choice to leave her family demonstrated her continuing lunacy and therefore could not be taken seriously.

The prosecution's strategy was more complicated. In the December 31, 1911, *Star-Telegram* story, Mrs. Boyce, as noted, had blamed Lena for Al's behavior. In some ways, this mirrored the defense approach to Lena's motives: Al was "hypnotized" by Lena and thereby rendered as incapable as she of making rational decisions. In court, however, Mrs. Boyce presented a more complex view, both of Lena and of Al, blaming Lena in some ways, but also indicating her belief that the confinement at Arlington Heights was cruel and unnecessary. Al was routinely excoriated in court, even by the prosecuting attorneys, who did not see any percentage in excusing his behavior. Only Harry Hendricks, speaking in summation for the prosecution, made any attempt to defend him:

A great deal has been said about Al Boyce in this case . . . and a great deal has been said in denunciation of him. It is natural in view of this testimony, we should all condemn him with more or less bitterness, but you can't say, because the curtain is drawn on that part of it, just what share of the blame should be borne by a married woman who participated in the wrong with him.

You have heard about his ranch on the Pecos and his ranch in Montana, and you know what limited experience he must have had with women. And you have heard Dr. Braswell testify that this woman was brilliant, gifted with reasoning powers beyond the average woman.[219]

The prosecution also spoke of Lena in ways that implied she was morally lax, although not morally insane. This probably occurred more than the papers indicate: Moral laxity was certainly the "subtext" of all the testimony regarding the Colonel's comments about her. A week or so after the mistrial was declared, Lena reported to Al that "at the trial the lawyers asked the jury if they supposed for one instant the Boyces wanted you to marry a woman as vile as me, a prostitute. . . . Papa followed the lawyers out + told them they would have to take it back that nobody could call me a vile woman—+ they said they didn't mean it that way."[220] The picture of Tom Snyder trailing the lawyers out to defend his daughter's reputation is a poignant one. Snyder's choice to back Beal, despite his initial anger toward him, was probably based on his desire to protect his daughter's reputation: Better the public should think her weak-minded than think her loose.

In an odd sort of way, this might have been the approach taken by the seven jurymen who voted to acquit Beal. Their Texan chivalry and masculine pride might have made it difficult to accept a viewpoint that blamed Lena for the behavior of the Boyce males. At the same time, married as most of them were, the idea that their wives might suddenly take a notion to leave them must have struck fear into their hearts. The defense did nothing to alleviate this fear and indeed encouraged it. Cone Johnson's comparison of Beal to Christ—which must have raised a few eyebrows even in 1912—probably resonated for those jurymen who saw Beal as truly martyred by a wife he loved enough to defend despite her betrayal of him. If they secretly thought she was as bad as the prosecution said, their sympathy for Beal's circumstances might have made them willing to grant him the "cover story" of insanity to explain and excuse her behavior.

What is missing in both viewpoints—Lena as "bad" or Lena as "insane"—is any recognition that a married woman might simply decide she no longer wanted to be married to her current husband. The issue of remarriage and divorce for women was of great interest in the 1912 climate of suffragism, socialism, anarchy, strikes, and all the other early twentieth century challenges to the status quo. The possibly serendipitous coincidence of a *Star-Telegram* feature, published on the same day as the account of the Colonel's death, illustrates this. Its subject was "How

Many Times Should a Woman Marry: Question Whether It Is Respectable for a Woman to Have an Unlimited Number of Matrimonial Affairs."[221] Several women gave their views.

The redoubtable Lillian Russell, "who, by some, is thought to be the most beautiful woman in America," weighed in on the subject on the eve of her fourth marriage. This, she hastened to explain, she regarded as her "second marriage" because her first "was a disappointment and mistake. My third was not a marriage. My second was, so I consider it my first and only one. Therefore, that which is called my fourth marriage will really be only my second." In a burst of early century optimism, she claimed that even though "[t]here are not many good men . . . because the world has not furnished the conditions for goodness in men . . . [i]t is beginning to do so." She concluded in exuberant metaphor. "When a man gets into the habit of excusing his rudeness by saying 'O well, she is just my wife'—why then, if the woman is one of modern spirit, the domestic ship tacks around and heads right for the divorce court."[222]

Russell's opinion was shared, though with far less charm of expression, by the Baroness Bazus, whose relative improvement in marital status was indicated by the notation "formerly Mrs. Frank Leslie." Eva M'Donald Valesh, "editor and lecturer," however, voiced a different point of view. "Frequent marriages," she opined, "suggest commercialism. . . . There is the flavor of barter and sale about [the woman who has had several husbands]. . . . Men are cleverer than women, and their ideas are written in the laws they have made governing marriage . . . instituted for the protection of posterity and to centralize property. Frequent marriages confuse children, so to speak, and scatter property. . . . In my opinion, women who marry often destroy the fine spiritual essence of femininity."[223]

Lying deeper even than the fear that for her own reasons a wife might decide to leave a marriage was perhaps a fear of female eroticism. This fear is indicated in part by the nature of the rumors surrounding Lena, as well as by the agitated debate over whether she was a "good" or a "bad" woman. It was the erotic heart of the story—the force of the attachment between Lena and Al and its fundamental nature—that both titillated and troubled people in 1912. Erotic love is, of course, a wild card in any time and place, particularly erotic love of the evident strength of Al's and Lena's. In the Texas of 1912, however, it seems to have been an especially charged subject. Even today, Lena's willingness to give up her daughters for the sake of her lover makes one uneasy. In 1912, in a culture just emerging from Victorianism, still tightly bound by traditional Southern views of femininity and faced with a rapidly changing world not far from the wrenching shifts brought about by the First World War, the idea of a respectable woman's erotic urges must have made people both curious and queasy. Convention made the "bad" woman the container for female sexuality; insanity might explain its presence in a "good" woman, who otherwise surely would never experience such feelings except possibly when well-confined to the marital bed and at her husband's bidding.

"The lack of absolute and sure control," wrote Kitty Barry. Whether it was Lena's control over herself or Beal's control over her, its absence seems to have frightened people. "I was taught," said my father, "that Lena lost control of her feelings." For that, his mother (my grandmother) looked down on Lena, as did many others. The siren song of the body and of the heart was to be resisted in all but the most appropriate circumstances.

Lena was well-aware of the depth of disturbance the trial had stirred up. Writing Al from her sister's home in Lake Charles, she comments repeatedly on the stength of public passion about the story: "You are so far away . . . you don't realize . . . the intense feeling over the affair—all Texas is divided over it."[224] Although she planned originally to rejoin Al in Canada, she was strongly advised against it by her attorney O.S. Lattimore, who told her that "not only Texas but the whole U.S. would tear up creation to find us—and that it would be impossible for us to go anywhere in Canada or a foreign country." With Lattimore's assistance, she planned to go to California instead, where he advised her to establish a legal residence and simply wait until feelings had died down and Beal might be willing to consider a divorce.

"I will die," she wrote Al from her sister Pearl's home in Lake Charles, "if I can't get away from this horrible talk. . . . if I even sit on the porch, people stop at the gate to stare at me—and it is killing me by inches—newspaper reporters come up here almost every day trying to interview me." The gossip was unrelenting and vicious. There was a report that she and Beal's brother, Joe, had been lovers[225] and an intimation that her daughters were illegitimate.[226] There was also the previously mentioned rumor so awful she couldn't bring herself to write it down for Al.[227] Possibly this involved nymphomania, since she did not understand the term when she first heard it,[228] and the word in 1912 lacked the currency it now has. As a diagnosis, nymphomania pathologizes Lena's eroticism in the extreme. If it was the rumor, it speaks clearly to the enormous fear the subject of her sexuality engendered.

Lena realized very quickly that Beal would never be convicted in Texas.[229] For all three principals, a waiting game with the highest possible stakes ensued. In Bassano, Canada, Al at first expected Lena to join him and, when that hope was dashed, tried to find the means to rejoin her in the States. Lena claimed Beal—awaiting his next trial—had told Billie Steele "he wouldn't be surprised to get a stray bullet any time."[230] On March 1, 1912, he hired a bodyguard, John Blanton.[231] He sold the house in Amarillo,[232] moving frequently with Blanton from Amarillo to Paducah to Plano and elsewhere, probably with some hope of making certain his trail would not be too easy to follow.[233] In all probability, since it was his neck, he did not feel as certain of the next trial's outcome as Lena did.

Lena had anticipated being accompanied to California by a woman (probably a cousin) she called Cootsie. She found instead that she was to be accompanied by Nellie Steele, Billie Steele's unmarried sister; Cootsie had been warned off by relatives who told her Lena was only going to California to make it easier to get to Canada.[234] Beal paid Nellie's way. The claim was later made that he had also paid Lena's,[235] but it seems very likely that he did not. Lena continued to inform Al of the economies she was taking to preserve the money he had given her[236] and wrote him that she was "pretty sure Beal is paying [Nellie Steele's] expenses," a statement that makes less sense if he were also paying hers. Led to believe that she would receive one hundred dollars a month from the sale of the house in Amarillo,[237] Lena evidently thought she could scrape by. "It costs almost nothing to live" in Los Angeles, she reported to Al soon after her arrival.[238]

Lena saw Beal and her children in Dallas just prior to her departure for California. Beal tried both to tempt and to threaten her: If she would promise not to see or communicate with Al, he would send her children out to California in June. If, on the other hand, she made one move toward rejoining Al, Beal would "follow [them] to the end of the world."[239]

All three principals were, to a great degree, hampered by the positions staked out by the other parties and by the legal situation as it existed in the spring and summer of 1912. Al could not easily reenter the United States. Were he to return to Texas, he might make the situation worse for his family. Beal's chances of being acquitted if he killed Al in Texas were high enough to incentivize, rather than discourage, that effort. And D.A. Atwell's attempt to indict Al on federal charges of white slavery continued to worry him, his family, and Lena.[240]

Lena, wisely advised not to try to get back to Canada, was stuck in California, where it quickly became apparent that her mail was being intercepted and opened. On April 17, 1912, she wrote Murray, the Canadian lawyer, saying she had not heard from Al since March 26. When she went to the post office to collect a registered letter Murray had sent, two blank sheets of paper fell out.[241]

Beal, having proclaimed in court his desire to rescue and protect Lena, had only limited options for enforcing her cooperation. He could not recommit her; he could not, in any obvious way, force her to live with him; and he could not kill her or beat her badly. What he did instead, judging from Lena's letters, was to draw the net ever more tightly around her so that her movements became more and more constrained. He watched her mail; he paid Nellie Steele's way to California to keep an eye on her; he made certain the children did not visit or communicate with her;[242] he denied her the money he'd promised from the sale of the Amarillo house; he kept her jewelry (shipped back from Canada) after he had promised to send it to her if she signed the release; and he gave away her household furnishings.[243] In short, insofar as was possible given the constraints his defense imposed on him, he created a climate of deprivation and intimidation, a climate that Lena's own guilt and fear made worse.

Lena's health had not been good in Lake Charles. She continued unwell in California, reporting that she was unable to eat, suffered from terrible headaches, back aches, pain, and insomnia.[244] These symptoms were almost certainly psychosomatic and reflected the terrible strain she was under. The letters to Al, taken in their entirety, paint the portrait of a highly emotional woman under extreme tension, whose mental health and sense of perspective both deteriorated significantly in California. Alone except for Nellie Steele, in a landscape and among people she did not know, away from Pearl's loving support, and hearing less and less from Al because of the watch on the mail, she became ever more frantic. "Precious you must think and think what is best for your poor miserable girl and I will do just as you say," she wrote Al on April 6, a theme repeated in many of the letters throughout this period. Afraid that Beal was planning to kill Al, she warned him:

[I]f he knew you were in Texas he wouldn't hesitate to hire someone kill to [sic] you or shoot you in the back—he carries two guns one a big automatic, he carries it in his front pocket + told me it would knock a man down fifty feet away—If he knew where you were + there is an indictment he would try + have you arrested + shoot you unarmed + John Blanton never leaves him one minute.[245]

By April 17, Lena reported to both Murray and Pearl that she intended to return to Texas, either to check herself into a sanitarium because of her health, or to go on to Lake Charles.[246] This seems one of the turning points in the story, and, in retrospect, a terrible decision. As a result, Al also returned to Texas, the very safest place for Beal to kill him.

3

Just prior to her departure from Los Angeles, Lena was surprised by a note from a man who, judging from her response, suggested a meeting and brought news from Al. (The note does not survive.) Though she believed it was too dangerous to meet with the go-between, she wrote that she would be at the Orpheum Theater that afternoon, where possibly he could slip her a letter from Al.[247] It is clear from the subsequent notes to Al that when she arrived at the Orpheum, she saw Al himself—for the first time since their final arrest in Winnipeg. They did not speak to each other.

On Sunday, April 21, Lena and Nellie boarded the train for Texas. From the hastily written notes from this period in the Boyce collection, it seems clear that Al and his go-between/bodyguard also boarded the train. That began a cat-and-mouse game wherein Al and Lena tried to communicate without raising Nellie's suspicions. At some point not clear from the correspondence, Al disembarked. Before he did so, however, he told Lena that he was going to stay in California. She could write to him, but he would not write to her anymore for the present, and he asked that she

destroy the letters he had written her, a request
with which she sadly complied.[248]

It is not entirely clear what lay behind Al's
request. Certainly, two considerations must have
been fear of the way Beal might use his letters if
he discovered Lena had them and desire to keep
his whereabouts hidden from Beal. Though Lena
was clearly frightened that Al intended to leave
her (a theme that recurs in the notes written
on the train[249]) by the time he disembarked, she
seemed to believe they had an understanding on
which to proceed. In an intriguing footnote in
The Flamboyant Judge, J. Evetts Haley writes:

*Al Boyce left the Panhandle and its tensions for a
visit with his distant relative, Ira Aten, the great Texas
Ranger and once-manager of the troubled Escarbada
Division of the XIT Ranch, who had retired to a
farm near El Centro, California. 'We expected Beal
to follow him out here,' Mr. Aten recalled, 'and, if he
had, we were going to kill him.'[250]*

Lena wrote to Al, under the pseudonym
of L.B. Ogilvie, first in Pasadena and later in
Heber, California. Heber is in Imperial County,
not far from El Centro and the Mexican border.
Though it is difficult to see how Beal would have
found out where Al was, since he was no longer
writing Lena and Al was coming from Canada,
it seems likely Al visited Aten at this time, as
Haley recounts. What is unclear is why Al
remained there: To lure Beal out to California,
to contemplate going into the cattle business
with Aten, to escape the Canadian cold, to plan

his next move, or to try, at his family's behest, to sever the relationship with Lena.[251]

Lena returned to San Antonio, saw her daughters and Beal briefly, then checked herself into Johnson's Sanitarium in Fort Worth.[252] In the fashion of this story, in which almost all the characters seemed to know or be related to one another, Dr. Clay Johnson, who owned the sanitarium, was related to Beal's defense attorney, Cone Johnson. Mildred Bridges, Lena's nurse at the sanitarium, was a Boyce family friend.[253] Lena believed she would be safe in the sanitarium and trusted her nurse to the extent of begging Al to write to her and enclose the letter in an envelope addressed to Bridges.[254] At last, on May 18, 1912, Lena received a letter from Al on the eve of what both regarded as their anniversary.[255] The wait without word from her lover had been painful. Evidently, Al expressed his suspicions about why Lena had seen Beal on her return to Texas and he may have chided her for not remaining in California with him. Lena responded:

Oh precious please don't misunderstand me, I have done all the time what I thought was best for you—I could never have seen you in Cal—I was never alone a minute the only time was the day I went to Long Beach to see if I had heard from you + Billie wired her [Nellie Steele] to watch me every minute . . . the last two days in Cal—she was so suspicious + saw me looking at the boy you had with you—+if I had staid [sic] out there it would have been dangerous for you. I told Beal I was coming here—he would have kept me from it if he could—but I knew you would be safe with me here. . . . Of course Beal has no control over me, + I could come back to Cal—but he would have my every movement followed—and watched. . . . you say it hurts you for me to see him—Precious I hate him so I almost go wild when I look at him. . . . I told Miss Bridges I must be an awful woman, but in my heart I wished he was dead—+ she said well we are alike for that is my wish. . . . [Beal] knows I'd die before I'd live with him again—and he had just as soon kill me as not.[256]

On May 21, 1912, Lena wrote another letter to Al in response to a letter that Al sent enclosing a letter from his brother, Henry—now informed of Al's whereabouts, possibly through Bridges. Henry had good news: Will Atwell would be forced to dismiss the white slavery indictment. No longer under danger of arrest, Al was now determined to return to Texas. Lena begged him not to come to Fort Worth, writing that she feared for his life if he did so. She advised him to go to Dalhart instead: "[I]f you go to Dalhart . . . no one can say you hunted trouble."[257] This letter of May 21, 1912, is the penultimate one in the Boyce archives; the last was written August 10, 1912. By that time, despite her protestations in her letter of May 18, she was living with Beal in Dallas.

What happened to cause this state of affairs and, indeed, what happened between May 21 and July of 1912 are another two mysteries of the story.

During the month of May, Beal kept moving, spending some of his time at his ranch in Paducah for roundup, where, according to John Blanton, he whiled away spare time with target practice.[258] Then, around June 20, something caused Billie Steele to take Lena from the sanitarium in Fort Worth to the Steele home in Dallas. Cross-examination questions to John Blanton suggest that he may have seen Al on the street in Fort Worth around this time.[259] Steele testified that, prior to collecting Lena, he had received information from Miss Bridges that led him to telephone Beal at Paducah. An objection by the State, sustained by the court, prevented Steele from testifying to the exact nature of the conversation he had with Bridges.[260]

What did Miss Bridges tell Billie Steele? That Al was back in Texas? That Lena and Al had been in correspondence? Given the degree of Lena's trust in her, Bridges' decision to contact Steele seems a vast betrayal. On the other hand, Bridges was never placed on the stand, which suggests that possibly her role was different, or her "information" more ambiguous than Steele's testimony implies. In any event, Beal met Steele in Dallas and was "considerably agitated and worried . . . over the news," whatever it may have been. He returned with Steele to collect Lena at Steele's home.[261] From there, Lena and Beal departed for San Antonio and spent the next few weeks traveling incessantly between Dallas,

Fort Worth, and San Antonio, staying in various hotels or at the Steele house. The children, now staying at Georgetown, probably with Beal's stepmother, occasionally joined them.[262] By July 8, 1912, Beal and Lena and their children had rented a flat at 4523 Reiger Avenue in Dallas.[263]

Why did Lena return to Beal? What persuaded her, after Bridges' conversation with Billie Steele, to leave the sanitarium? In her last surviving letter to Al, Lena wrote that she knew "how it has hurt you me being in the same house with him—But oh, do you remember you wrote me you wouldn't write me anymore—and when I didn't get your letters."[264] A report printed in the *Star-Telegram* on September 21, 1912, said Lena told "close friends" that she had returned to Beal for her children and money, two entirely plausible reasons.[265] With Al out of communication, perhaps the strain of living apart from her children—who, according to Blanton, were brought to Johnson's to visit her at least twice[266]—coupled with the fears that Al was going to leave her and the evident, if unspoken, guilt she manifested in her physical symptoms, led her to agree to live again with Beal. In any case, as with the decision to return to Texas from California, it proved a terrible mistake, leading, with the steady march of destiny, to her lover's death.

By the end of June, or the beginning of July at the latest, Al was back in Texas. Lynn Boyce testified that Al was In Fort Worth starting about

July[267] and Blanton may have seen Al in Dallas at the end of June.[268] The night clerk at a Fort Worth hotel testified that Al was registered there, under the name of L.B. Moss, from July 17 to August 1, 1912.[269] Thus, by July of 1912, the three principals were nearer one another than they had been since early January of 1912, when Lena had been deported from Canada. But this time, they were in Texas, where people had none of the Canadians' finicky scruples about a man's need to use his gun to defend home and family.

At about the beginning of July, Blanton's employment with Beal temporarily ended. Beal told Blanton he no longer required his services,[270] which makes little sense, since, if anything, Beal had more need of a bodyguard now that Al was back in Texas. Blanton hinted at what may have been the real story when, during cross-examination, he said he quit. He denied that he had ever given the following explanation to an acquaintance in Fort Worth: "No, sir, I did not tell [Mark Raley] that Albert Boyce had come back to this country and Sneed was going to kill him, and I was afraid he would lay it off on me and that was too much for seventy-five dollars a month."[271] Somehow, the denied quote makes more sense than anything else. By the beginning of August, however, Beal had rehired Blanton, but only to guard the children because Blanton apparently refused to "go with" Beal.[272]

In the ensuing weeks, while Beal and Lena were at the Reiger Avenue house, everyone's behavior gives the impression of people verging on hysteria. Lena chose, almost incomprehensibly, to make confidants of her upstairs neighbors, a Mrs. L.A. Rogers and her sister, Mrs. C. Castleton. Mrs. Rogers became a stellar defense witness after Al's murder. While some of her testimony strains credulity, the fact that Lena showed her and Mrs. Castleton letters from Al and that both women mailed and received letters for Lena seems indisputable.[273] (The lovers were by now destroying each other's letters after reading them.[274]) After her bad luck with her brother-in-law John Pace and again with Miss Bridges, Lena's confidence that her upstairs neighbor ladies would keep their mouths shut can only be explained by the lengthy strain she had been under.

Al visited Pearl in Lake Charles briefly. Then, on July 21, while Beal was gone and Lena's mother was in an upstairs bedroom of the Reiger Avenue house, Al spent the night with Lena.[275] She had often expressed the desire to have Al's child and on this night, according to her letter of August 10, she became pregnant.[276] Al returned to Amarillo shortly afterward.[277]

About July 23, Beal showed Billie Steele a July 19 letter that Pearl had written to Lena from Lake Charles. Pearl encouraged Lena to come with "her babies" to Lake Charles and said she was "crazy about" Al. Beal was "too big a coward," she continued, to stand up to the officer Pearl proposed to get to stay at the house if Lena should come.[278] It is unclear how Beal got the letter. It is also unclear whether Lena ever saw it, and why, once Beal was aware of it, he did not immediately choose to take Lena off to his brother Marvin's farm in Milam County, as he did a few weeks later.

In fact, the entire decision to leave Reiger Avenue and the basis for it—or rather, the added basis for it, since there seems to have been sufficient reason previously—is mysterious. On August 13, Beal suddenly made up his mind to take Lena and the girls to the Milam County farm, located on the other side of the Brazos River from Calvert, where Marvin Sneed and his wife Cara had their home. Lena was very upset by the decision to leave Reiger Avenue and did not know where she was to be taken. At her request, Mrs. Castleton phoned Al in Amarillo to tell him what had happened.[279] Al wired Pearl asking her to meet him in Dallas because "am informed Sneed has again locked Lena up." A sympathetic Western Union official wrote Beal, enclosing a copy of the telegram.[280]

Mrs. Rogers testified that after Beal made the decision to leave Reiger Avenue, but before his departure, she told him about an aborted plot to kill him. According to Rogers, Al had written Lena a few days earlier, relating his failure to find Beal on the train Lena had indicated he would be riding. Al had been joined by two other men, whose names Mrs. Rogers could not recall. All three were masked—"nobody on Earth could have identified us," she claimed Al wrote—and they were "fixed for" Beal.[281]

Mrs. Rogers' testimony about this plot is so ludicrous that one is tempted to dismiss it altogether. First of all, as the state attorney was quick to recognize, it was hard to explain the fact that Mrs. Rogers knew about the plot but did not inform Beal until well after its failure:

"Now you tell the court that Mrs. Sneed was in your house plotting murder and you did not tell your husband about it?"

"I wanted to tell him and he would not listen."

"And she was there plotting murder, and you did not tell the officers about it?"

"Why no, I did not want to get mixed up with it."

"And plotting murder and you did not tell the man about it whom you regarded and cared for in a sort of a brotherly way?"

"I told him that night—the day they left [to go to Calvert]."

"If you felt this sisterly interest in it, as you said . . . why didn't you tell him before?"

"Well I was afraid to get mixed up in it. I didn't want to have anything to do with it."

"What caused you not to have any fear when you did tell him?"

"They were ready to go and I thought . . . well when they go away, I will be through with it. I won't see them anymore or won't have anything to do with it."[282]

(Mrs. Rogers' sister, Mrs. Castleton, did not

testify, indicating perhaps that her loyalties remained with Lena as—despite her testimony—Mrs. Rogers' also seem to have been originally.)

More damning still to Rogers' testimony, however, is the nature of the alleged plot and the language she quotes Al as having used to describe it. It is difficult to believe that three masked men wandering through a train would not arouse deep suspicions in Texas, where train robberies were fresh memories. And regardless of how well-disguised he was, Al would naturally have been the very first suspect if Beal had been killed. But it is Mrs. Rogers' repeated insistence that Al wrote that he saw "no one of that description"—meaning Beal—on the train, which strikes the falsest note. Al would hardly have needed a description of Beal to recognize him unless Beal himself was traveling disguised, of which there is no evidence.

And yet, the lovers certainly must have been desperate by July of 1912. An earlier plan to join each other during Beal's upcoming trial[283] had apparently been abandoned or put on the back burner, perhaps because it was clear that Beal would hire people to keep an eye on Lena. Whatever Lena's motivations in rejoining Beal, Al's increased suspicion, hurt, and anger must surely have been one of the results. Prior to his trip to California, someone had apparently told Al that Beal had circulated a report that he and Lena were reconciled.[284] "I will kill myself before I live with him,"[285] she had assured Al on the train, yet here she was, living with him again.

One can easily imagine that Lena—at first frightened that Al's silence in California meant he was leaving her, then frightened that he would be killed in Texas, and perpetually anxious over her children and money—chose to return to Beal and then became equally frightened that Al would believe she no longer loved him. This might partly explain the pregnancy: It was a child she wanted and what better way to prove her love for Al and make certain he would not abandon her.[286] In any case, her letter of August 10, 1912, indicates that the lovers were, as Rogers' testimony suggested, hoping that Beal would go to Amarillo.[287] A telegram surviving in the Boyce Collection also corroborates some of Rogers' testimony. Dated August 8 and addressed to Al at his mother's residence, it reads: "Mailed letter yesterday to address given think abstract was sent last night not positive. Morgan." The "abstract" is almost certainly Beal himself and "Morgan" a code name for one or both of the sisters; Mrs. Rogers testified that Mrs. Castleton called Al after Beal took Lena away and used the name "Morgan" to identify herself.[288] Lena wrote in the August 10 letter that "Mrs. C. [Castleton] went to town + sent the telegram to you for me,"[289] an apparent reference to the "abstract" telegram.

The subject of killing Beal had come up in Lena's notes to Al after they had been arrested in Canada. In one she wrote, "[I]f they bring you back [to Texas] I want you to kill Beal."[290] Yet in another note she wrote just after Beal's arrival in Canada, she rejects the idea: "[D]arling I don't want you to kill B or him you as [it would be] an awful thing + I will have to answer to God for it."[291] Thereafter, through March of 1912, there is nothing to indicate any plan to kill Beal in Lena's letters. They are instead concerned with keeping Al out of reach of Beal or a killer he might hire. A letter of April 6, 1912, questioned Al:

What did you mean by saying you would go to Texas as soon as the next trial was over—I think I know what you mean—I notice what you said precious about longing to give Beal every chance to kill you—I don't want you to give him one chance— and don't you take one chance for my sake—If he knew you were in Texas he wouldn't hesitate to hire someone kill to [sic] you or shoot you in the back.[292]

Al was reputed to be the "crack shot" in the Panhandle.[293] Lena's question perhaps indicates that he imagined an encounter with Beal along the classic, though infrequently actual, Western lines: Beal might draw on him, Al would draw faster, kill Beal, and be able to claim self-defense. Perhaps it was a version of this that Aten and Al dreamed up when Al was at the Aten Ranch in El Centro.

The final evidence indicating a plot to kill Beal is the comment Lena's sister Pearl made in the letter that Beal acquired: "I don't think the Jack," she wrote, referring to Beal, "is long for the world."[294] That letter, as noted, was written immediately after Al had visited Pearl in Lake Charles.

Ironically, then, almost the best evidence against a plot is the absurdity of Rogers' testimony that one existed. Yet, it seems quite probable Lena and Al were hoping for a confrontation that would end in Beal's death. Did Al hope to ambush Beal and, if so, how did he expect to get away with it? Was he planning to lure Beal into a face-to-face test of gunslinger skills? Had he perhaps reached the stage where any conclusion, his own death or Beal's, was preferable to the torment he was suffering, both over the separation from Lena and the guilt over his father's death and his mother's wrenching fear and sorrow? Mrs. Boyce was reported to have taken him out to view his father's grave at Llano Cemetery. "There," she said, pointing to a spot in the ground, "is your place."[295] Everyone knew the business was not finished.

And now, with Lena and the girls on the farm in Milam County, the endgame began. From Calvert, John Blanton took the train to Dallas, where he stayed a few days. There, he ran into Joe Barr, an appropriately named bartender. Barr had recently seen Al and his friend Lucien Hughes, who were staying at Dallas's Southland Hotel.[296] Barr testified that when he had visited Hughes in their room, he saw a "regular arsenal . . . there were six or seven six shooters around the room, automatic[s]."[297] Blanton testified that on his return to the farm, he told Beal about Al and Hughes and that Al had been by the Reiger Avenue house after the Sneeds had left.[298] Beal stopped shaving.[299]

Blanton's role is curious and another of the enigmas of the story. Lena's letter of August 10 indicates she trusted him, though Al did not, and some of Blanton's cross-examination hints at the state's belief that his loyalties were more complex than his presence as a defense witness might indicate. The state poked at his contention that he went to Dallas just "because he wanted a few days off."[300] Did he go to Dallas at Beal's behest to try to find Al? One doubts it, as he seems to have wanted to stay clear of any attempt to murder Al. Did he go because Lena asked him to try to contact Al? If so, why did he claim he told Beal about Al in Dallas? Was he playing Lena for a fool the whole time, operating as a kind of double agent who fed all the information he could get from her back to Beal? If so, some of what he knew never surfaced in Beal's trial. Did self-interest prevail and persuade him to testify in Beal's defense when there were no other sensible options? The last, whatever preceded it, certainly seems likely.

After Blanton returned, Beal left the Sneed farm. He traveled first to Fort Worth, where, bearded and wearing blue "goggles," he registered at the Mansion Hotel under the name of John Wilson.[301] There, he met with one of his attorneys[302] and asked Beech Epting, a tenant farmer from the Paducah property, to come to

Fort Worth. According to Epting, once he arrived in Fort Worth, Beal told him he wanted to shut down his business operations in Amarillo.[303]

By September 9, 1912, Beal, Epting, and Al were all in Amarillo.[304] Al had come to town from Dalhart a few days earlier and was staying with his mother at the Polk Street house.[305] Under an alias and in disguise, Beal rented a room from a Mrs. T.E. McKibben for a few nights.[306] Subsequently, he occupied a cottage across the street from the Polk Street Methodist Church, that Epting, also using an alias, had rented for him.[307] On September 10, Al went out of town for a few days with his brother Lynn to look at land around Groom.[308] Beal and Epting covered the cottage windows with shades nailed wrong way around. They left a little space between the shade and the sill at the bottom of the window and cut a hole through the bottom of the screen. Then, they pushed a bed against the wall so one could peer out that small opening they'd created and get a view of the street.[309]

Late at night on Friday, September 13, Al returned to Amarillo.[310] He and Lynn had gotten Lynn's auto stuck in the mud, and Al went out the next morning to help Lynn retrieve it. That afternoon, Al left his mother's house to head downtown, as was his custom when he was in town.[311] It was September 14, 1912, nine months and a day since the death of his father.

At Polk and Eighth, Al spotted Ernest Robinson—minister of Polk Street Methodist,

SNEED, TE

Sneedville, Texas, south of Paducah, the hub of Beal Sneed's Cottle County agricultural interests. Circa 1912. Willie and Gene Conway, who operated the "ranch store," stand in the center of the porch.
Photo courtesy of Gene Fowler.

who had presided over the Colonel's funeral—returning with some groceries to the parsonage. Perhaps the encounter was awkward for both men. "Howdy-do," Al said. Robinson returned the greeting and made a remark about the weather cooling. "Yes," said Al, "it's getting to be fall of the year."[312]

And then Beal emerged from the hide-out cottage with a shotgun in a wooden case. He dropped the case and began firing before he reached the streetcar rail.[313] He fired three times, aiming first to disable Al's trigger hand. According to Earl Jackson, a young boy who witnessed the murder, Al realized just quickly enough what was happening to plead, "Don't shoot me. Please don't, don't."[314] Dr. Robinson claimed Al never said a word.[315] Jackson also testified that Beal walked up to the curb and shot Al again, saying afterward, "I guess you are dead, you son of a bitch."[316] This account was also contradicted by Robinson,[317] but Jackson, who in the excitement had run his bicycle into a hitching post and fallen into the mud, seemed to suggest that the minister might have missed something because he was running up the parsonage steps "as fast as he could" once the shooting started.[318]

Al twitched for a time on the sidewalk where he had fallen, but never spoke again.[319] He had an undrawn Luger semi-automatic pistol tucked into his belt.[320] In a short time, about fifteen people had gathered around him. A C.J. Collier found two letters in Al's coat. One, as yet unstamped, was addressed to "either Mrs. or Miss Snyder" in either LeGrange or New York; Collier could not remember which, although they do not seem like easy destinations to confuse. The other letter was addressed to Al in blue type and had been opened.[321]

Mrs. Boyce arrived very quickly, shaking her fist and crying out:

'[S]how me the man who killed this man,' or words to that effect and someone asked her if he could do anything for her, and she said all she wanted was to see the man who did the killing and reached over and brushed his hair back and said something about if only her boy could speak to her, and reached over and got the letter addressed to Mrs. or Miss Snyder . . . and she held it folded in her hand. Mr. Speed told her not to interfere with the body . . . but I heard no reply from her.[322]

Al was dead by the time he was brought to his mother's home. The doctor counted thirty pieces of shot in his body and then stopped counting.[323]

Meanwhile, Beal coolly walked north on Polk Street, even greeting an acquaintance who failed to recognize him.[324] Outside the Magnolia Hotel, where at the time the artist Georgia O'Keeffe (just beginning her stint as a teacher in Amarillo) was staying,[325] a man asked him "What is the trouble?" "Nothing," Beal replied. "I have got him."[326] O'Keeffe and some other guests watched him continue on his way to the jailhouse, where he turned himself in.

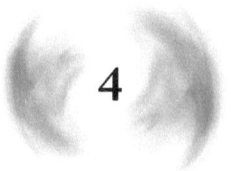

4

Al was buried on September 16 in the spot his mother had pointed out to him at Llano Cemetery. The Reverend Ernest Robinson officiated. Al's brothers William, Henry, and Lynn, served as active pallbearers, as did Lee Bivins and Ed Farwell, among others. The honorary pallbearers included former Sheriff J.E. Hughes, Judge S.T. Fagan, Frank Harrington, R.E. Stalcup, and W.E. Farr.[327]

On September 21, the *Star-Telegram* published an account of Lena's reaction to her lover's death: Heartbroken, she had told "close friends" that she loved only Al and had returned to Beal because of her children and money. Though it is unclear who Lena's "close friends" were—her sister, Pearl, is certainly a possibility—the report seems genuine, Lena's only apparently voluntary effort to set the public record straight. Perhaps she felt safe to do so since Beal was in jail in Amarillo awaiting his habeas corpus hearing. Also on September 21, Joe Sneed Jr. arrived in Amarillo and passed the Boyce boys in the street without incident, thereby calming fears of further trouble.[328] On September 23, Beal's habeas hearing began.

Although there were three more trials, including the trial of Epting as an accomplice, the story, insofar as the public was concerned, had reached its climax. There was, of course, great interest in new details about it all. Beal's disguise, the "death cottage," his initially unknown accomplice, the revelations that Mrs. Rogers' testimony provided about Lena's contact with Al during the summer of 1912, and the publication of letters Al wrote in Canada at the beginning of the year, were highlights of the newspaper stories after his death. Nonetheless, the combined coverage of the three remaining trials took up less print in the *Star-Telegram* than coverage of the first.

It was clear there would be no more shooting. Joe Sneed Jr. and the Boyce brothers had met peacefully in the streets of Amarillo. Henry Boyce recognized that his mother simply could not take any more deaths. The enmity between the families would not result in an old-style feud. The twentieth century had come to Texas and despite the many features of the story that are reminiscent of frontier justice, Texas was no longer the frontier.

In many ways, though the murders were executed in a fashion that seems to belong to an earlier era, one recognizes in Beal's savvy use of high-priced lawyers, the newspapers, public opinion, "spin-doctoring," and the legal system itself, behavior that seems indubitably to belong

103

to our own times.

It is fascinating to realize that almost every issue that arose about the conditions under which Beal's trials were held remains an issue in high-profile cases today. How could an unprejudiced jury be gathered after so much pretrial publicity? Was it right that so much money should be spent trying a wealthy man? Was it right that the defendant should have access to such high-priced legal help? Was it possible to shorten the length of time it took to try a case like this one? Texas in 1912 was a world in which newspapers were the only media at work, $25,000 was a lot of money, and two and a half weeks was a long time for a trial. That world may seem simple compared to our own. The people who lived in it, however, struggled over the same kind of problems, though at vastly different scale, that we struggle over today.

Judge J.N. Browning denied Beal bail in Amarillo on September 28, 1912,[329] but was reversed by the Appeals Court in Austin on October 30, 1912.[330] The six weeks Beal spent in jail awaiting bond were the longest he was ever incarcerated because of the killings.

Beal's second trial for the killing of Colonel Boyce began November 11, 1912. The defense again requested that the trial be moved out of Judge Swayne's courtroom,[331] a motion the judge again refused. Beal had arrived in Fort Worth a few days earlier, looking "fresh as a daisy" and heavier than he had been on September 14.[332]

The Boyce and Sneed clans were again ensconced in their respective hotels—the Sneeds at the Siebold, the Boyces at the Westbrook.[333]

In many ways, of course, the second trial followed the evidence and strategies established in the first. Certain aspects, however, were streamlined. Judge Swayne, evidently convinced a guilty verdict was appropriate, tightened up on courtroom procedure and evidence. Concerned about jury tampering, he instructed the talesmen who arrived at the courtroom to "knock down and spit on" anyone who tried to talk to them about the case.[334] He also told the completed jury that he would no longer allow their wives to hug and kiss them in the courtroom, a move which probably did little to increase his popularity.[335] The second jury was much in the mold of the first. All were married men ranging in age from twenty-three to fifty-six; all were Southern born and reared, with Tennessee representing the northernmost point of origin among them.[336] During the selection process, defense attorney McLean had rejected a venireman born in New York. "Too far north," was McLean's damning comment.[337]

This time around, Judge Swayne disallowed testimony that quoted Colonel Boyce's comments about Lena (such as W.H. Fuqua and others had given in the first trial[338]), though he permitted a witness to describe the comments as "vulgar, obscene and defamatory."[339] Swayne also disallowed the use of Beal's letter to W.H. Fuqua;

the Boyce telegrams introduced as exhibits in the first trial; and Ed Farwell's testimony regarding the check Al had written to Lillie Flowers prior to his elopement with Lena.[340]

The defense introduced a W.A. Weaver, who testified that, as Beal entered the Metropolitan after supper, the Colonel said, "There comes the ___ ___ ___ now."[341] Weaver was conclusively shown to have been nowhere near the Metropolitan the night of the killing. He was charged with perjury, but the use of a clearly impeached witness seems to have had little negative effect on the defense. Beal's former neighbor, a young man named Ernest Thompson—son of L.O. Thompson, the owner of the drugstore where some of the "man talk" about Al and Lena had occurred—testified that Beal had remarked on a train that he "ought to kill" the Colonel. Apparently, this also was not deleterious.[342]

The *Star-Telegram*'s descriptions of the people who attended the trial provide an interesting indication of the nature of public interest. On the day Tom Snyder testified, more than the usual number of elderly women showed up in court.[343] At the noon recess on November 21, many women shook Beal's hand. On the day Beal was scheduled to testify, a large portion of his audience were girls ten to fifteen years old accompanied by adult women.[344] The implications are mysterious and fascinating. Had Beal become something of a teen idol before such creatures were a fact of life? Or did the older women want to show their young charges the sort of man they ought to set their minds on when they began searching for a mate? Whatever the reasons, the feminine presence in the courtroom when Beal testified during the second trial seems to indicate that Beal had won the battle of public opinion as much with women as he had with men.

On December 3, 1912, Beal was found not guilty of the murder of Colonel Boyce, despite Judge Swayne's instructions to the jury that they must convict him of murder in either the first or second degree and his specific exclusion of self-defense or manslaughter.[345] The jury reached agreement on the first ballot taken December 2, but it was too late to go home, so they waited until the next morning to report their verdict to the judge. On hearing the words "not guilty," Beal "emitted a cowboy yell." His lawyers, busily writing out the appeal they expected to have to file after Judge Swayne's instructions, were utterly surprised.[346]

The following report on the reasons for the verdict appeared in the *Amarillo Daily News* on December 4, 1912:

Foreman J.D. Crane explained why they acquitted Sneed today. 'The best answer is because this is Texas. In Texas, we believe in protection of the home at any cost. We in Texas believe a man has the right to safeguard the honor of his home, even if he must kill the person responsible.'

The "because this is Texas" line is, of course, irresistible, but it is worth noting that the *Star-Telegram*'s version is considerably less dramatic. Crane's comment is preceded by Cone Johnson's remarks to a group of jurors:

'This may go in the North, but thank God, it hasn't reached the South yet.'

'No,' Crane replied, 'this is Texas.'[347]

Were it not for the garbled grammar in the remainder of the Amarillo version of Crane's statement, one might be convinced that a newspaperman had massaged his words into something with just a little more punch.

In any case, the point is not only clear, but accurate. The jurors, and presumably much of the public, perceived acquitting Beal as a statement in favor of the values of home and family as Texans, and Southerners generally, saw them. The murder of the Colonel became a blow struck against challenges to those values brought by the new century, challenges that Johnson and McLean tied directly to the North: Free love, divorce, lightness among women, and the failure of honor. It may not be stretching the point too far to say that the defense implicitly encouraged the jurors to consider the "unwritten law" in the case as it applied to three "homes": Beal's, the jurors' own, and the state of Texas. For the Anglo jurymen, living in a state culturally suffused by recollections of the Civil War and Reconstruction, the connections were no doubt easily made.

The Amarillo paper and the *Star-Telegram* also differed in reporting Lena's reaction to the verdict. "Afterwards," claimed the *Daily News,* "it was announced that Sneed and his wife . . . had become reconciled. Heretofore, they had been living apart, and she refused to testify, it was alleged, in his favor. 'I am so glad,' she was reported to have replied when Beal called her with news of the verdict at her hotel in Fort Worth, 'Can't we leave here tonight?'"[348] The *Star-Telegram's* version claimed that it was the clerk in the lobby of the Court Hotel who told her of the verdict: "Mrs. Sneed smiled faintly. 'Is that so?' she asked, quietly, with no display of emotion."[349] She caught sight of a reporter and hurried back to her rooms. The paper then quoted a telephone call Lena made to Beal at McLean's office during which she asked him, "Are we going away tonight?" and he replied, "I don't know. I will be down at the hotel in half an hour and let you know." How the reporter managed to hear both sides of the conversation is unclear.

"Sneed's relatives" denied that Lena had been "closely guarded," said the *Star-Telegram*. "'She has been free,' they were quoted, 'to come and go as she wished. . . . She is not under guard and anyone who wanted to see her could do so.'" A reporter suggested that the experience of the newspapermen was different. "'Of course,' replied the unnamed relatives, 'she doesn't want to talk for publication. She is happy over the verdict and loves her husband and her

Sneed family men present at Beal Sneed's trial for the murder of Albert G. Boyce Jr., Vernon, Texas. February 1913. Front row, from left: Sneed brothers Joe T. Jr., Beal and Harold Marvin. Back row: Joe Barton (cousin), J.W. Sneed (uncle), Tom Snyder (father-in-law), H.C. Beal (uncle).
Photo from the author's collection.
Identifications courtesy of Joseph H. Pool.

children.'"[350]

Obviously, once Beal was acquitted of the murder of the Colonel, few could have expected that he would be convicted for the murder of Al. But before Beal's third trial, Beech Epting was tried for acting as his accomplice. Epting's trial was widely regarded as a dress rehearsal for Beal's.

Epting's case was taken up on January 6, 1913, in Memphis with Judge J.A. Nabers presiding. The defense, composed of Beal's usual team as well as some local counsel, requested a continuance until after Beal's trial, arguing that if Beal were acquitted of murder, Epting could hardly be charged as an accomplice.[351] Memphis was a small town, and its resources were strained by the trial. Private citizens were asked to open their homes because there were not enough hotel rooms for the lawyers, reporters, family members, and veniremen who came into town. Excluding the trial itself, entertainment was scarce, with dominoes til 10:30 p.m. at the hotel the usual extent of it.[352] Once the trial was underway, Judge Nabers permitted the jury to see "The Rosary" at the Memphis Opera House after investigating the play and then lining the jurymen up "on the courthouse lawn and [making] them swear they would not be influenced by anything they would see or hear."[353] The winter cold was acute.[354]

Nabers denied the motion for continuance, and jury selection began. A talesman was found who had never heard anything of the whole affair, the only such instance in all the legal actions.[355] Epting pleaded not guilty. A hotel clerk in Quanah, where Epting had fled after the killing, testified that Epting had told him he had witnessed the shooting.[356] Epting, however, claimed that Beal had misled him and that he knew nothing of the plans to kill Al.[357] The defendant's wife and six children, aged two to eleven, appeared in court, the children "littering the floor with ginger cake crumbs."[358] Because he was indicted for the same offense, Beal was not permitted to testify for Epting.[359]

In their closing arguments, the local prosecutors, H.H. Cooper of Amarillo and S.A. Bryant of Hall County, became the first to picture Al as Lena's protector and to defend their love affair:

'Any woman would rather live in a hovel with a man she loves than in a palace and all its splendor with a man she hates,' said Cooper.

'I never heard it argued before that because a woman is married to a man, she becomes his slave and chattel. Mrs. Sneed was slammed from sanitarium to sanitarium just because she loved another man than her husband. If Al Boyce did love her, as his letters indicated, what manner of man would he have been not to respond to her call for him to rescue her.'[360]

Bryant's argument followed similar lines: "They say she is insane just because she didn't love Sneed for giving her a fine home and diamonds. She was a bird in a gilded cage. She was born in a land of freedom and she yearned for the freedom that was rightfully hers."

Roland Brown of Paducah spoke in Epting's defense, making an interesting argument in favor of the "unwritten law." Jacob's daughters had been seduced by the princes of the tribe of Hamor. When Jacob's sons found out about it, they killed not only the seducers, "but all but wiped out their tribe and . . . God protected them." District Attorney Spencer objected to the reference, arguing that Brown "was not quoting an authority." "It seems to me," responded Judge Nabers, "that the Bible is high enough authority."[361]

Epting was acquitted in thirty minutes on January 23, 1913.[362] The Boyces and the prosecutors could have had no illusions about the results of Beal's upcoming trial. In fact, no one seems to have had any. The newspaper coverage is thin indeed, compared to that of the first trial, or even to the other two. When jury selection began on February 11 in Vernon, with Judge Nabers again presiding, veniremen were, for the first time, asked directly their opinion about Beal. Most of them sympathized with him and several veniremen were excused "because they said they believed the unwritten law higher than any written law." One of the few who said he thought Beal ought not to go free, a Vernon jeweler named N.R. Heath, was, upon expressing his opinion, asked by McLean, "Wait a minute . . . where were you born?" "Pennsylvania," replied Heath. "I thought so," was McLean's response.[363]

The jury—completed in two days—consisted of the same sort of men who had served on the others: Mostly married, mostly fathers, all born in the South.[364] The preponderance of evidence had been introduced in the other trials or at Beal's habeas corpus hearing, although the defense made an effort to prove Beal had not been disguised at the time he shot Al.[365] The state, naturally, laid great emphasis on the premeditated nature of the killing while the defense once again claimed the protection of the "unwritten law" for Beal's act. According to the *Star-Telegram*, the defense also pointed to a "Supreme Court ruling," which held that, regardless of the amount of time that had elapsed since the alleged transgression, a husband could not be convicted of first degree murder for killing a man who had bedded his wife, if he killed him the very first time he saw him after he learned about his wife's infidelity. Whether spurious law or inaccurate reporting, the "Supreme Court ruling" doubtlessly riled the Vernon jury's sensibilities on Beal's behalf.

The defense also, ironically, mounted a temporary insanity defense for Beal. This was presented by two Vernon physicians whose qualifications were not of the highest.[366] Dr. J.E. Dodson had formed his opinion by listening to Beal's testimony, while Dr. D.C. Darnell believed that Beal, like Lena, was morally insane, but he somewhat diluted his diagnosis on cross-examination by claiming that statistics showed that "about eighty percent of all people are morally insane."[367]

Beal testified in his own behalf and related that after he had taken Lena and the children to the Milam County farm, he came to Fort Worth and telephoned Epting. "These people had taken all I had but my little children and they were still trying to kill me, and something just took me to Amarillo," he testified.[368] As reported in the *Star-Telegram*, Beal's version of Lena's interlude at Johnson's sanitarium and her return to the Steele house in Dallas ran thus:

She told [Beal] at the Johnson sanitarium in Fort Worth, where he had placed her after he returned, that she had cried for him every night she had been away from him. She said she had the baby's shoes about her neck all the time and a picture of him. The Sneeds went to San Antonio after Mrs. Sneed had been hurried from the Johnson sanitarium to the home of Billy [sic] Steele . . . in Dallas when Steele learned Al Boyce was in Fort Worth.

'In San Antonio,' Sneed said, 'I told my wife that this man was back in this country and I said, you know that one of us must die. If I am killed, send the children to Georgetown, where they will be safe.'[369]

Beal testified that Lena and the children were in Waco, "that he and Mrs. Sneed [had] not lived together as husband and wife since the elopement, and that he was caring for her as he would a sick child."[370] The fact that his Valentine's Day cards came only from his children underscored his contention.

"Do you now believe that your wife is mentally deranged?" McLean asked him.

Sneed faced the jury and spoke with deep feeling in his voice.

"I know it, gentlemen," he said, "better than I know I'm living. That is all that has kept me in the world—just to care for and protect her."[371]

The defense continued to hammer at Al's

115

character. Joe Barr testified again about the arsenal that Al and Lucien Hughes had in their hotel room at the Southland and about their visits to the saloon where Barr worked. Though the newspaper did not report it, one may assume that Barr's testimony and cross-examination were similar to those in the habeas corpus hearing. There, emphasis was laid on the fact that Barr told Blanton that he supposed Al and Lucien were in town "on a drunk." Barr testified that Lucien was "drunk two days while he was in town," so drunk that Barr was nervous about him "monkeying around with those automatics."[372] Barr did not testify that he ever saw Al drunk, but Barr may have had less-than-stringent standards on the subject. He claimed he was not drunk himself on the night he visited with Lucien, although he had had "eight or ten drinks since two-thirty in the afternoon"[373] and testified that he always had "two or three drinks in the morning before breakfast."[374]

During the habeas corpus hearing, the defense had also presented testimony about Al's stay at the Dixie Hotel in Fort Worth during the summer of 1912. Questions about the location of the Dixie, in the notorious Acre, were evidently intended to suggest something about the nature of a man who would stay in such a hostelry.[375]

That Al drank, at times "hard," seems undeniable. Judging from Lena's letters to him, the subject had come up between them, and he had evidently tried to go on the wagon. At one point in February 1912, she tried to contact him in Canada and, hearing nothing for several days, became frantic, finally receiving word that he had been "very sick."[376] In the next letter that survives, she wrote:

I want to write about you being sick—but oh Albert I can't—It almost killed me but my love for you is my very life—and I love you just like you were my own little child and could never lose faith in you—and I know the temptation was awful. And that you have suffered as much as I have from it—and oh precious heart I know you won't ever do it again— . . . and darling I thank God you didn't drink very much. . . . I won't say that it didn't hurt me . . . but oh Albert I could never be mad with you—and where a woman's love is her life there is no need to ask forgiveness.[377]

In her surviving letters, the subject comes up only once more between them. Lena wrote of a promise Al had apparently made to her on the subject:

[Y]our word and promise . . . is all I want—for you are honor itself. . . . Don't ever think I don't realize the horrible temptation. . . . I have never written about it before precious heart, because to me your promises are sacred—but I want you to know how I understand, God bless you.[378]

Lena repeatedly emphasizes Al's honesty and honor in comparison to Beal's. Indeed, the tone of Al's letters, his evident generosity with Lena, his return to his mother's house because she expressed her desire that he "comfort [her] in her sorrow,"[379] his silence and coolness among those who were not intimates, his handiness with a gun, and his preference for ranch life create the impression of a man who in another context might well be celebrated for exemplifying a Western masculine ideal. Indeed, his liquor and cigarettes fit right in with the stylized view of the cowboy. In another of the ironies of the case, it is Al, rather than Beal, who seems most deeply to exemplify the style and values of the Old West, though it is Beal's acts that initially most remind one of them.

By this point in the case's progress through the courts, there was little interest in pursuing leads that might alter the story as everyone now expected it to unfold. Judge Nabers refused to allow in evidence a letter (in Al's possession at the time of his death) written to Beal by an Earl McFarland. The *Star-Telegram* reported that attorney Willmut Mitchell Odell questioned Beal about this letter, in which McFarland asked "for money for alleged services. Sneed said he turned the letter over to his lawyers and did not know that it had ever been in the possession of Al Boyce . . . [that] he didn't pay McFarland any money."[380] This letter has survived in the Boyce collection and the nature of the "services" is quite specific:

My object in seeing you was in regards to the settlement made by your attorneys for my services rendered in your case.

Your attorneys told me to come + after having a talk with Mr. Scott, also Mr. Johnson they told me to go *ahead with my plan which I did, + that you know of. I told Mr. Johnson that I had an agreement to pay the juror $100. He said that would be satisfactory. My expense there, train fare + hotel bill for 23 days came to $76.00. When the settlement was made Mr. Scott gave me $150.00 saying that was all you had allowed. Which made me $26.00 looser—[sic] regardless my time.*[381]

Beal was, years later, convicted of bribing a juryman[382] in a case of far less importance, so it certainly does not seem out of the realm of possibility that he would have considered such tactics when his neck was at stake. But Judge Nabers seemed uninterested in going any further down this particular legal alleyway.

Mrs. Boyce, on the stand for the last time, protested bitterly against the judge's instructions that she only answer the questions put to her. "Then this is just a trial for the living," she exclaimed, "and there is no trial for the dead. Why can't I tell the whole story as Captain Snyder did? He hasn't had the sorrow and the trouble that I have. I can't cry, but my heart is dripping blood."[383] She claimed that Beal had known of Al's infatuation with Lena before she and the Colonel did, but her assertion was not pursued, at least not according to the *Star-Telegram*'s report.

Though Rugh H. Cooper, a private prosecutor, claimed that "Mrs. Sneed's love for Boyce was genuine and that Boyce's love was true,"[384] McLean argued in his summation that "[w]henever a home is despoiled, gentlemen, I say there ought to be a killing."[385] Walter Scott concurred: "The best shots ever fired in Texas . . . were the shots that took Al Boyce's life, and I hope every home destroyer in the land meets the same fate."[386]

On February 25, 1913, after three minutes of deliberation, the jury found Beal Sneed not guilty of the murder of Al Boyce Jr. The jury had received the case at ten o'clock the night before, and only one man had been on the fence. He had changed his mind during the night. One juror said the verdict would have been the same if the defense had not presented a single witness. "He said that about all the prosecution had proved was that Sneed killed Boyce, and they knew Sneed admitted that, and they had a general idea of Sneed's provocation." None of the Boyces were in court when the verdict was announced.[387]

Out at Llano Cemetery, among the laudatory epitaphs for many of the Boyces—"Peace, perfect peace," "She lived for others," "Faithful to every duty" (the Colonel), "Faithful to every trust" (Mrs. Boyce)—sits the stone at Al's grave. "Jesus knows all about our struggles," it reads. Even a casually astute observer, knowing nothing of this story, could intuit something tragic had happened, just by looking at the inscriptions and the dates. One can imagine Mrs. Boyce, laboring over the choice of epitaph. Mrs. Boyce, who outlived every one of her children as well as her husband, stricken by grief and aged beyond her years, searching for the words that would both acknowledge and forgive Albert's fault.

Reconciled in at least some fashion by the time of Beal's final acquittal, Lena and Beal remained married for the rest of their lives. The years were hardly free of notoriety thereafter, though nothing remotely as dramatic as the events in Amarillo and Fort Worth occurred again. In the early twenties, Beal engaged in periodic shooting matches in Paducah with a man named C.B. Berry. Berry had shot Georgia Beal's husband, Wood Barton, to death in a dispute over payment of some Black men hired to pick cotton. Despite a number of encounters, neither Beal nor Berry was killed. Both were tried for shooting at one another, and both were acquitted of the charges.[388]

At the start of August in 1924, Beal began a nine-month stint at the federal prison at Leavenworth. At last convicted of something, he had been found guilty of attempting to bribe a federal petit juror in a land dispute case in which he was involved. The bribery methods were crude. Beal and his codefendant. J. Renfro, had shared whiskey with the juror, an H.J. Patterson, in Renfro's room in an Abilene hotel. After a few drinks, the two offered Patterson one thousand dollars to "hang" the jury. Despite an appeal, Beal's conviction in this case stood. And despite numerous personal appeals to United States

**Beal Sneed, right, accompanied by Ray
DeBoice on Polk Street. Amarillo 1948.**
Photo courtesy of Joseph H. Pool.

senators and representatives, to the United States attorney general, and even to President Herbert Hoover, Beal was forced to serve some time. It must have come as a quite a shock.[389]

Beal and Lena made their permanent home in Dallas beginning in 1923. Beal died on April 22, 1960, and is buried In Hillcrest Memorial Park.[390] Lena died on March 6, 1966, and is buried beside her husband.[391] Neither obituary in the *Dallas Morning News* breathes a word of the scandal that defined them both half a century earlier.

The story has continued to withhold the solution to its greatest mystery: What happened to Lena's pregnancy? During the many conversations we had on the subject, Mrs. Tripp said that Thomas Thompson believed Lena visited her sister Pearl at the conclusion of Beal's trial in Vernon. If she became pregnant in July 1912, she would have been close to full term by March 1913. Did she have the child in Louisiana with Pearl's doctor husband in attendance and give it up for adoption? Mrs. Tripp says that Thompson heard that a boy was born and survived until he was five or six. Sneed relatives have never heard anything about such a pregnancy. Pearl's grandson, A.J. Perkins, can account for all those buried in the Perkins plot in Lake Charles, so it seems unlikely that Pearl raised the child until its death.[392] Birth records were notoriously inaccurate in the early twentieth century and in cases where obscuring the circumstances of the birth was desirable, records were sometimes not made. It is, of course, possible that Lena somehow obtained an abortion after Al's death, though it is difficult to imagine her willingly terminating the last physical link she had to her lover. It is also possible that—as she seemed prone to when upset—she miscarried relatively early. In any case, though she was reported "shortly to be a mother" in the September 26, 1912, edition of the *Star-Telegram*, there is never another public mention of her pregnancy. As with so much in this tale, silence is the only answer.

EPILOGUE

It is probable," wrote the correspondent reporting on the end of Beal's trial for killing Al, "that no other case of a similar character has occupied so much space in the public prints of the country, a fact attributable to the prominence of both the families so intimately involved."[393] And yet, shortly thereafter, it was as if it had never occurred, at least as far as public discussion went. I have always heard that Mrs. Boyce simply forbade her remaining sons to kill Beal, thus preventing a full-blown feud. If this story has a heroine, it is certainly she, who had the strength of character and force of will to insist that the killing stop. When Beal was convicted of bribing the juryman, Sneed rumor had it that the Boyces were behind the conviction. If so, it must have been cold comfort to them.

Why was this story so taboo for so long as a matter of public discussion? Even in the 1990s, although most everyone I met was extremely cooperative and interested in my project, I became aware—through the attempts of some of my Amarillo contacts to line up interviews for me—of several older women who were "horrified" that I was writing about "the feud." Most had not even been born at the time the killings occurred, but they had inherited the enveloping code of silence.

It is interesting that this trend toward silence began almost immediately after Al's killing. The

Amarillo newspaperman covering the scandal remarked that "[t]he people have ceased in a great measure to talk about the affair, as it is painful to friends of all parties. Where soon after the tragedy, there was a seeking of conversation regarding the same, at present there is in many instances a distinctive shrinking from a mention of the subject that is visibly so painful and distasteful."[394]

Of course, some of this silence was protective, not only of the parties involved, but of the public peace. C.L. Sonnichsen writes that "the feud history of Texas is almost unknown to the average Texan. . . .Western reticence is at least partly responsible for this condition. The old-time Texas pioneer was close-mouthed, particularly about other people's troubles and weaknesses, and besides, it was once dangerous to talk . . . If nobody talks, the feud may be 'lived down.'"[395]

The Boyce family remained in and around Amarillo for decades afterward. So did the Thompsons—the family of Beal's sister Georgia. So did Joe T. Sneed Jr.'s family. (As noted, Beal and Lena moved to Paducah and then to Dallas.) In Amarillo, people close to the Boyces or the Sneeds kept their mouths shut, at least in public. I am told one could not be friends with both families; one had to choose sides. Never were both invited to the same party.

Perhaps the silence went deeper, however, than protectiveness toward the families involved. One senses that the subject was traumatic beyond any fears of renewed trouble. One of my contacts, speaking to one of the women who was horrified by my interest, asked her why she felt so reluctant to talk. "Well, honey," she replied, "we just didn't take destroying a woman's reputation lightly."

Amarillo is, despite its size, a close-knit town. As in all such towns, its residents possess much intimate knowledge of each other. Its prominent families frequently stretch back deep into the city's short history, and the sense of the past clings more tenaciously in Amarillo than is often true elsewhere. In this sense, the Sneed-Boyce "feud" remained "live" past the point it might have in a town more distant from its roots. One senses Amarillo's secret life, things hushed up, or, to put it another way, stories at once known in the private sense but unknown in the public one. Perhaps some of the trauma generated by the Sneed-Boyce saga continued to involve its heart: An erotic attachment between Al and Lena so great that they were not willing to continue to abide by the rules of their public positions. They were "good" people from "good" families. They were supposed to act like it. If Lena had been willing to remain married to Beal while taking Al as a lover, people might well have accepted it as part of Amarillo's secret life, even if they did not approve. It was Lena's insistence on "spilling the beans," her doomed effort to make her private feelings and her public position correspond with each other, that led to the trouble. Who knows

127

what might have happened had she succeeded in freeing herself from Beal? The relationship with Al would certainly have altered to include the more tedious and less exalted aspects of domestic love. It may even have foundered. But one comes to believe she truly loved him. It is difficult to see any other good reason for her to have behaved as she did.

The choice to return to Beal was probably made on far more pragmatic grounds. Her father and most of her family were in favor of it. Beal was a hero to many. She would lose her children if she left him. Her reputation was in shreds, and Beal's position as her husband somewhat protected her. Last, but certainly not least, what would she do about money if she left?

In the subterranean chambers of the mind, however, there are many motives beyond the practical. Perhaps, deep down, Lena had experienced a profound failure of nerve beginning during her stay in California, despite being a woman whose force of will and personality was evidently vast. And perhaps there was also a subtle way in which returning to Beal served as a strange memorial to Al. If she left Beal, being the sort of woman she was, full of erotic energy and attraction to and for men, she would have become involved with someone else. She would have had to go beyond Al. Perhaps she did not want to. So she stayed with Beal, content to invoke the third, vanished point of the triangle by keeping the other two points in place.

She did not, by all accounts, give Beal an easy time of it. One joke goes that his punishment was getting her. But one cannot help liking her: So much energy, so stubbornly determined to get what she wanted; manipulative, yes; a liar at times; funny; sexy; "smart as a whip;" impulsive to a fault, perhaps, at least once upon a time.

There was, of course, an element of denial in the Amarillo treatment of the business. But there was also an element of respect—an acknowledgement that the forces involved were powerful and best handled carefully.

Shortly before his death in 1995, I spoke with Alward White, a good friend of Thomas Thompson, and at one time an attorney for many of the prominent families in town, including that of Beal's sister, Georgia Thompson. He told me he had graduated from Amarillo High School in 1935. At his fiftieth high school reunion, Lillian Blanche Brent, Georgia Thompson's daughter, had approached Albert Boyce, one of Al's nephews and father of the man with whom I have become friends. She stuck out her hand. "Albert," she said, "this thing's been going on a long time and neither one of us had a thing to do with it. I think it's time it ended." They shook. "As far as I know," said Mr. White, "that was the end of it."[396]

ENDNOTES

1   Mary Kate Tripp considers the *Fort Worth Star-Telegram* account to be the most complete of the existing newspaper coverage, as did Thomas Thompson. It is indeed comprehensive. The Amarillo paper frequently quotes *Star-Telegram* stories verbatim, though often not in full; in addition, Amarillo editions are often missing for particular days. The story was covered on a national level, but accounts in papers such as *The New York Times* indicate the scope of public interest in the story rather than providing accurate or in-depth coverage. The habeas corpus transcript survived because it was the only related court action that Beal Sneed lost, at least initially. After the murder of Al Boyce Jr., Judge James N. Browning denied Beal bail in Amarillo. Consequently, a transcript of the hearing was made and forwarded to the appeals court in Austin. My call to the district court in Fort Worth in 1996 confirmed that transcripts do not exist for Beal's two trials there. Mrs. Tripp heard a transcript had been made of Beal's trial in Vernon, despite his acquittal, but the Wilbarger County Courthouse burned and all records were destroyed. My calls to the Hall County Courthouse and to Cecil Langford, the court reporter in 1996, confirm that no transcript survives of the related Epting trial held in Memphis.

The process of making transcripts was far more laborious in 1912 than it is at present. Consequently, the habeas corpus transcript is clearly not "verbatim" in the sense that one would now use the word. Attorneys' questions, for example, are sometimes left out if the context of the answer makes it clear what the question must have been. There are also typographical errors which, for clarity, I have corrected.

2   J. Evetts Haley, *The XIT Ranch of Texas and the Early Days of the Llano Estacado* (Chicago: Capitol Reservation Lands, 1929; Norman: University of Oklahoma Press, 1969. 1985), 217.

3   Richard F. Selcer, *Hell's Half Acre, The Life and Legend of a Red-Light District* (Fort Worth: Texas Christian University Press. Chisholm Trail Series, no, 9, 1991), 235.

4   Details of the killings, which will be expanded on later, are taken from the *Fort Worth Star-Telegram* accounts and testimony in the habeas corpus hearing of John Beal Sneed.

5   Mary Kate Tripp, telephone interview with author, Amarillo, Texas, November 1993.

6   C. L. Sonnichsen, *I'll Die Before I'll Run, The Story of the Great Feuds of Texas* (New York: Devin-Adair Co., 1962; Lincoln: University of Nebraska Press, Bison Book Edition, 1988), 288.

7   John Beal Sneed testimony. John Beal Sneed vs. The State of Texas, Potter County. Application of Writ of Habeas Corpus, Habeas Corpus Hearing no. 1535, District Court of

Potter County, Judge James N. Browning presiding, p.198. Hereinafter cited as Sneed Habeas Corpus Transcript. Photocopy of transcript from the private archives of Joseph H. Pool of Amarillo, Texas, hereinafter cited as Pool Collection.

8 D. H. and J. W. Snyder are mentioned in numerous books and articles. For thumbnail sketches of both see: John M. Sharp, "Experiences of a Texas Pioneer," and D. H. Snyder, "Made Early Drives," in *The Trail Drivers of Texas*, ed. J. Marvin Hunter, (n.p.: Cokesbury Press, 1925; Austin: University of Texas Press, 1985) 721-729; ibid 1029-1031.

9 Sneed Habeas Corpus Transcript, 198.

10 Haley, *XIT Ranch*, 217. See also: Lewis Nordyke, *Cattle Empire, The Story of the 3,000,000 Acre XIT* (New York: William Morrow & Company, 1949; New York: Arno Press, 1977), 247.

11 "Long Illness Fatal to Mrs. Mary Boyce, Pioneer Amarilloan." *Amarillo Daily News*, 20 July 1929. Photocopy from Pool Collection. Microfilm available at Amarillo Public Library, Amarillo, Texas. Mrs. Boyce's first name was Annie, rather than Mary, and in all other sources I have found, including her epitaph, she is so named. William Boyce, another of Colonel Boyce's great-grandsons, confirmed in a phone interview with the author in January of 1997 that the correct name is Annie.

12 "Former Wacoan, Old Trail Driver,

Recalls Death of Sam Bass in 1878," *Waco News Tribune*, 3 December 1933. Photocopy from Pool Collection.

13   Haley, *XIT Ranch*, 82; Nordyke, Cattle Empire, 128.

14   Mary Whately Clarke, "Plains School Was Hobby of Panhandle Ranchman," *The Cattleman* (April 1953) 76. Photocopy in Pool Collection.

15   Obituary of Mrs. J. Beal Sneed. *The Dallas Morning News*, 7 March 1966. Photocopy in Pool Collection. I have always heard that Al attended Southwestern as did his brothers William, Lynn, and Henry, according to their obituaries. Because his brothers attended, it seems reasonable to assume Al did also, but I have been unable to confirm this. The formulation in Lena's obituary—that she "was educated at Southwestern"—tends to support the idea that she did not graduate. This formulation is also used in Lynn's obituary, whereas William's states that he "attended and graduated with honors from Southwestern University." As Lynn and Al seem to have been more interested in ranching than in school, it seems likely that Al also merely "was educated" at the institution. Obituaries for the Boyce brothers are as follows: "Judge William Boyce Dies; Son in One of Texas First Families," *Amarillo Daily News*, 5 January 1929; "Linn [sic] Boyce, Pioneer Plains Stockman, Dead," *Amarillo Sunday News*. 6 February 1927; "J. Henry Boyce, Pioneer Texas Cowman, Dies," *Amarillo Sunday*

News-Globe, 26 May 1929. All photocopies from the Pool Collection.

16   "Funeral in Dallas for John Sneed," *Amarillo Sunday News-Globe*, 24 April 1960. Photocopy from Pool Collection.

17   Harry N. Brandall, *Art Souvenir of Amarillo. Queen City of the Plains* (Amarillo: Harry N. Brandall. 1909), n.p. in the Bush Collection, Amarillo Public Library. Amarillo, Texas.

18   City-provided paving began in early 1911. The streetcar system, established in 1908, was the only one of its kind in the Panhandle at the time. Della Tyler Key. *In the Cattle Country. History of Potter County*. 1887-1966, 2nd ed. (Quanah-Wichita Falls: Nortex Offset Publications, Inc., 1972), 169, 214.

19   Local option elections were a common feature in Amarillo for the first thirteen years of the century. Control swung back and forth between the wets and the drys, with the drys winning the day in 1913. Key, *Cattle Country*, 178. For discussions of local option elections and Amarillo attitudes at the time towards liquor see *Faces of Amarillo*, videotape, Larry Benton and Lynn Hoke, Producers, Larry Benton, Director; "Insulation," program 6, sequence 1; "Refinement," program 4, sequence 3; "Standards." program 4, sequence 2; "Transportation." program 8, sequence 1. (Amarillo: Amarillo College Television Production, 1987).

20   For information on Amarillo during

this period see: B. Byron Price and Frederick W. Rathjen, T*he Golden Spread: An Illustrated History of Amarillo and the Texas Panhandle*. (Northridge, CA: Windsor Publications. Inc. 1986); Key. *In the Cattle Country*; The *Faces of Amarillo* series; Thomas Thompson, *The Ware Boys: The Story of a Texas Family Bank* (Canyon, Texas; Staked Plains Press, 1978); Ray Franks and Jay Ketelle, *Amarillo Texas: The First Hundred Years—A Picture Postcard History*, and *Amarillo Texas II: A Picture Postcard History* (Amarillo; Ray Franks Publishing Ranch. 1986 and 1987 respectively); J. D. Hamlin, *The Flamboyant Judge, The Story of Amarillo and the Development of the Great Ranches of the Texas Panhandle*, eds. J. Evetts Haley and Wm. Curry Holden. (Canyon, Texas: Palo Duro Press, 1972). The Hamlin book is notable for including the only account of the affair written by a contemporary who knew the three principals.

21 The Boyce house was situated down the street from the Lee Bivins house, which has survived and serves now as the headquarters of the Amarillo Chamber of Commerce. For a view of this section of Polk Street, known during this period as Silk Stocking Row, see Franks and Ketelle, Amarillo. Texas, postcard 12, and for examples of individual houses, postcards 46-57. The Curtis house (postcard 53), mostly closely resembles in style both the Boyce and the Sneed homes as they were pictured in the *Fort Worth Star-Telegram*, 9 February 1912. Microfilm, University of Texas at Arlington

Library. Arlington. Texas. The Boyce house was moved in the 1960s and restored, but was eventually demolished. See *Amarillo Globe Times*, 20 February 1962. Microfilm (Amarillo Public Library, Amarillo, Texas).

22 Sneed Habeas Corpus Transcript, 199. Information verified in Amarillo City Directory, Amarillo Public Library, Amarillo, Texas.

23 Mary Kate Tripp, letter to author on 27 November 1993, recounting gossip Thomas Thompson heard from Lena's former neighbors.

24 The issue of Beal's relative financial stability is an interesting and ambiguous one. Reported initially as a "millionaire banker and cattleman" (*Fort Worth Star-Telegram*, 27 December 1912), Beal certainly maintained a lifestyle that suggested wealth. Sneed family lore, however, indicates that he borrowed heavily from his relatives to pay the costs of his defense, which, according to my father, Joseph Tyree Sneed III, was never entirely repaid. The *Star-Telegram*, 16 December 1912, estimates the cost of Beal's defense at from ten thousand to twenty-five thousand dollars prior to both the Epting trial in Memphis, whose costs he apparently bore, and his own last trial in Vernon. Beal's letters written shortly after his final acquittal indicate a man who is dancing fast to keep his feet from the fire, trying to arrange loans on property in Paducah at favorable percentages. Letters of John Beal Sneed to J. T. Sneed. Jr. and W. H. Fuqua, 17 March 1913; and to T. Sneed Jr., 25 March 1913.

Photocopies from Pool Collection.

But the public most certainly perceived him as a wealthy man. *The Childress Post*, quoted in the *Star-Telegram* 10 February 1912, expressed astonishment that Beal's trial for the death of the Colonel had begun so promptly: "The killing occurred on Jan. 13 and the trial was begun in less than two weeks, notwithstanding the defendant did all that wealth and influence could accomplish to defer the trial. Considering the uniform ease with which attorneys usually get bad cases deferred or continued, it has been a general surprise that this rich man was forced into trial so soon. [I]t has long been the rule that men of wealth can have their trials put off indefinitely. Sneed ought to be tried just like a humble citizen and the humble citizen ought to have the same chance as Sneed."

25   Sneed Habeas Corpus Transcript, 233.

26   See "Capt. T. S. Snyder, Cattle Man, Dead," *San Antonio Express*, 1 March 1934. Photocopy in Pool Collection, for a description of Tom Snyder's ranching interests outside of Georgetown, where his family stayed.

27   Mrs. Tripp and I have had numerous conversations on the subject on Lena's and Beal's marriage; she has made this point frequently in the course of them.

28   John Beal Sneed testimony. Habeas Corpus Transcript. 201-202.

29   *Fort Worth Star-Telegram*. 15 September 1912; Hamlin, Flamboyant Judge. 94.

30   Mary Kate Tripp, interview with author, Amarillo, Texas, May 1994.

31   Sneed Habeas Corpus Transcript, 197; report of Tom Snyder's denial of earlier affair in *Fort Worth Star-Telegram*, 16 September 1912.

32   *Fort Worth Star-Telegram*, 20 November 1912. Supporting the idea of a long-standing attachment, however, was testimony about remarks the Colonel made in a train on 3 January 1912. According to both H. M. Walden, a cashier, and W. T. Johnson, president of the First National Bank of Denton, the Colonel remarked that the relationship had gone on for twelve or thirteen years, in other words, about as long as Lena's marriage. *Fort Worth Star-Telegram*, 20 and 21 February 1912. If so, the affair must certainly have been attenuated by distance, as Al was indisputably in Montana and elsewhere prior to his return to Amarillo. Mrs. Boyce, in contrast, testified that she had noticed nothing wrong between the two until the fall of 1910. *Fort Worth Star-Telegram*, 19 February 1912.

33   Nordyke dates the move around 1888. Nordyke, *Cattle Empire*, 180. Haley reports Al working on and presumably living at the XIT in 1894. Haley, *XIT Ranch*, 177. Beal testified that the Sneeds had moved to Georgetown in January 1889, and that the Boyce family was then living "just across the street and a half block east." Sneed Habeas Corpus Transcript, 197. Lena was born in 1879 or 1878—her tombstone says the latter. Elsewhere, I have assumed 1879 to be the correct date. Beal was born in 1877; Al in 1875. If the Boyces moved to Channing in 1889, Al would have been fourteen and Lena ten or eleven, certainly too young for a serious courtship. Dating the move in 1894 makes Al nineteen and Lena fifteen or sixteen, an entirely different matter.

34   In the one mention Lena makes of the state of her marriage prior to Al's return to Amarillo, she remarks, *"Can't* see now darling *why* I couldn't ever be happy with him—I did try so hard at first to be a good wife to him + please him—but it was his iron will—+contemptible dirty ways that he tries to hide that killed all the feeling over four years ago I ever had for him." (Lena's emphases). Letter of Lena Snyder Sneed to Albert G. Boyce Jr., 23 April 1912, private collection of Albert G. "Pete" Boyce, the great-nephew of Albert G. Boyce Jr. Hereinafter cited as Boyce Collection. Lena Snyder Sneed hereinafter cited as LSS; Albert G. Boyce Jr. hereinafter cited as AGB Jr.

35   Lena's birthday listed as 15 August 1879; Beal's as 30 December 1877; Al's as 24 July 1875.

36   Sneed Habeas Corpus Transcript, 293. As it was entirely in Beal's interest to prove that the elder Boyces were aiding and abetting the love affair from the start, the idea that Mrs. Boyce encouraged Al to borrow books from Lena may be spurious. On the other hand, Mrs. Boyce may have quite innocently suggested something along these lines.

37   Harold Bell Wright, *The Shepherd of the Hills*, (n.p.: A. L. Burt. 1907; Thorndike, Maine: Thorndike Press, 1982).

38   LSS to AGB Jr., 18 May 1912, Boyce Collection. Lena's language in this letter leaves little doubt that a physical consummation occurred a year earlier. She speaks of their "anniversary" and of "giving herself" to Al. Both Al and Lena regarded their union as a marriage, at least in their hearts. They exchanged rings sometime during their elopement. The ring Lena gave Al survives in the Boyce Collection, and is engraved with the words "Forever, Lena" on the inside. Lena's ring was lost in January 1912 when Beal pulled it off her finger and threw it out the train window on the way to Fort Worth to return her to the sanitarium. LSS to AGB. Jr., 10 March 1912, Boyce Collection.

39   Sneed Habeas Corpus Transcript, 205.

40   Ibid, 205-206.

41   Ibid, 211. Note, however, that this may be interesting more as an example of the way the defense portrayed Lena than as an accurate quote.

42   The newspaper restrictions are indicated not only by the refusal of the *Star-Telegram* to print the exact nature of remarks such as those W. H. Fuqua claimed the Colonel made, but also by comments Lena made in letters to Al where she mentions the amount of information that came out during various court actions which was not printed in the newspapers. LSS to AGB

Jr. 21 February 1912 and 6 April 1912, Boyce Collection.

43 *Fort Worth Star-Telegram*, 9 February 1912.

44 Sneed Habeas Corpus Transcript, 203-204.

45 *Fort Worth Star-Telegram*, 19 February 1912.

46 Ibid., 10 February 1912.

47 Ibid.

48 Report of testimony of Henry Boyce. *Fort Worth Star-Telegram*, 17 and 18 February 1912.

49 Ibid.

50 Ibid. Joe Sneed. Jr. was very close to the Boyce family. He was good friends with both Al and Henry and, in family lore, was engaged to marry their sister, Bessie, before her untimely death. See also Hamlin, *Flamboyant Judge*. 97; he served as a cashier and owned shares in the Amarillo National Bank when the Colonel controlled it, prior to its acquisition by the Wares, ibid., and Thompson, *The Ware Boys*, 43. With regard to Beal's trials, it is worth noting who did *not* testify; Joe Sneed. Jr was a notable omission. His absence from the witness list was probably due to his extreme closeness to the Boyces before the trouble, as well as his knowledge of the nature of the relationship between Al and Lena prior to the dale Beal claimed he found out about it. Since the defense made much of the fact that the Boyces had known about the affair for some time before October 1911 and had not informed Beal, it was no doubt awkward that Joe had also known about it. By contrast, the prosecution certainly avoided Joe for the obvious reason that he was Beal's brother. In the division of loyalties along strict family lines that characterized the trials, Joe could be counted on to ally himself with his brother.

51   LSS to AGB Jr., 6 April 1912, Boyce Collection.

52   Arlen Cohn, M.D., interview with the author, Berkeley, California, November 1996.

53   There were, of course, other times prior to the court action to which Lena referred in her 6 April 1912 letter when she might have become pregnant. Most notable of these opportunities was after 8 November 1911, when she and Al eloped, and before 27 December 1911 when they were arrested. Yet, had a miscarriage occurred at that time, the statement "and that it was you"—meaning, apparently, that Al was the father—makes no sense. In all probability during that time, he would have been the father. At the very least, there was no doubt that he was sexually intimate with Lena. Had a miscarriage occurred during the three weeks Lena was in the sanitarium before the elopement, one imagines there would be some evidence she had been confined to bed, or ill during her stay, which there is not. In fact, Dr. Allison, who owned the sanitarium, testified that she was a great deal of trouble because she was always wanting to go

142

places and do things. *Fort Worth Star-Telegram*, 19 January 1912. This leaves only the period between the time she was arrested and deported and her own habeas hearing on 19 January 1912. As with the Canadian sojourn, the comment "that it was you" makes little sense in this context. Also, in her letter of 9 January 1912, Lena wrote: "Mr. Pace asked me today if there was anything the matter with me, said I was so miserable and anxious to get back to you—I told him no, but I wish there was"—LSS to AGB Jr., 9 January 1912, Boyce Collection. Pace seems to be inquiring whether she is pregnant, and she seems to be certain she is not. As she was evidently the kind of woman who knew almost immediately when she did get pregnant, there seems little chance she was wrong when she talked to Pace. LSS to AGB Jr., 10 August 1912, Boyce Collection.

54 *Fort Worth Star-Telegram*, 31 December 1911. In the comments published in this edition, Mrs. Boyce said Lena told her she had asked Beal for a divorce prior to a conversation she had with Mrs. Boyce in July 1911. In an account of Mrs. Boyce's testimony published on 22 February 1913, the *Star-Telegram* reports that Mrs. Boyce said Beal knew about the infatuation before she and Colonel Boyce did.

55 Ibid., 7 February 1912 and 19 November 1912.

56 Ibid., 17 February 1912, report of cross-examination. Note that the habeas corpus transcript, which included Beal's direct testimony from the Fort Worth trial, does not include his cross-examination.

57   Ibid.

58   Ibid., 7 February 1912.

59   Sneed Habeas Corpus Transcript, 206. Interestingly enough, the testimony that Al informed Lena that J. T. Sneed Sr. was planning to tell Beal was not reported in any of the newspapers that I read. The testimony provides Lena with more of a motive for suddenly deciding to tell Beal than the newspaper accounts do.

60   Sneed Habeas Corpus Transcript, 207. Beal's effort to kill Lena is probably the best evidence that he had been totally surprised by her desire to leave him. It's difficult to imagine what else would have caused such a violent reaction unless he found out suddenly about a miscarriage and realized things had gone much further than he thought.

61   Testimony of Joe Sneed Sr., *Fort Worth Star-Telegram*, 7 February 1912; of Tom Snyder, 7 February and 19 November 1912; and of Mrs. A.G. Boyce, 19 February 1912.

62   Sneed Habeas Corpus Transcript, 209.

63   *Fort Worth Star-Telegram*, 7 February 1912.

64   Sneed Habeas Corpus Transcript. 209.

65   Ibid., 213.

66   *Fort Worth Star-Telegram*. 10 February 1912. Dr Turner is also listed as the former superintendent of Southwestern Insane Asylum and Arlington Heights.

67 Sneed Habeas Corpus Transcript, 214-216; see also *Fort Worth Star-Telegram*, 10 February 1913, for an account of Dr. Turner's testimony.

68 DIALOG Database: Dissertation Abstracts On-line; synopses of the following: John Starrett Hughes, "In The Law's Darkness: Insanity and the Medical-Legal Career of Issac Ray, 1807-1881" (Ph.D. Diss., Rice University, 1982); John Ellard, "The History and Present Status of Moral Insanity," *Australian and New Zealand Journal of Psychiatry*. [22] (December 1988): [388-389]; Allen D. Spiegel, "Temporary Insanity and Premenstrual Syndrome; Medical Testimony in an 1855 Murder Trial," *New York State Journal of Medicine* (September 1988): [482-492]; Herbert C. Modlin, "The Anti-Social Personality," *Bulletin of the Menninger Clinic* [47] (March 1983): [129-144]; S.P. Fullinwider, "Insanity as the Loss of Self: The Moral Insanity Controversy Revisited," *Arizona State University Bulletin of the History of Medicine* [49] (Spring, 1975): [187-101]); Lewis Aubrey. "Psychopathic Personality; A Most Elusive Category," *Psychological Medicine* [4] (May 1974); [133-140]; Bernard L Rotenberg et al. "The Biblical Conception of Psychopathy: The Law of the Stubborn and Rebellious Son," *Journal of the History of the Behavioral Sciences* [7] (January 1971): [29-38].

In Joe Pool's correspondence is a letter written to him on 15 March 1971 by Norman Nadel, then the cultural affairs writer for the Scripps-Howard newspapers. It reads, in part:

"I was reading Irving Stone's new biographical novel on the life of Sigmund Freud. 'The Passions of the Mind.'... Do you recall when we were discussing your murderous great-uncle, you said that his wife had been put in an asylum for a time on the grounds of 'moral insanity'? . . . Well, back in Vienna of the 1870s and 1880s, and probably earlier as well, 'morally insane' and 'moral insanity' were in both legal and medical use, to describe a criminal whose crime was somehow sexual in nature, such as a rapist or molester, probably, or any of the other varieties of deviates. However, it apparently was a wrap-up term, to cover any situation they couldn't identify otherwise. Krafft-Ebbing apparently was one of the first psychologists to try to get society to accept the evidence that such people might be sick, mentally, as well as criminal, and should be treated, rather than just locked up. . . . At any event, it was a bum rap for your great-aunt, as well as a misuse of the term, even by standards of the time."

Those who saw the film *Tom and Viv* may recall that Vivian Heigh-Wood, T. S. Eliot's first wife, was diagnosed as morally insane in England during the 1930s. The doctor in the movie describes the disease as almost epidemic among women of a certain high social class who suddenly begin behaving in socially unacceptable ways.

69   Sneed Habeas Corpus Transcript, 214.

70   Ibid., 216.

71   Ibid., 218.

72   Ibid., 216-217.

73   Quoted in *Fort Worth Star-Telegram*, 14 February 1912.

74   Ibid., 17 February 1912.

75   Sneed Habeas Corpus Transcript, 224-225.

76   *Fort Worth Star-Telegram*, 8 February 1912, gives details on LSS and Flowers and report of Ed Farwell's testimony.

77   *Fort Worth Star-Telegram*, 8 February 1912.

78   Sneed Habeas Corpus Transcript, 247.

79   *Fort Worth Star-Telegram*, 19 February 1913.

80   LSS to AGB Jr., 8 March 1912, Boyce Collection.

81   Ibid.

82   Letter of AGB Jr. to LSS. 15 January 1912. Sneed Habeas Corpus Transcript. 253.

83   AGB Jr. to LSS, 13 January 1912, ibid., 249.

84   LSS to AGB Jr., 23 April 1912, Boyce Collection.

85   LSS to AGB. Jr.. 2 March 1912. ibid.

86   AGB Jr. to LSS, 13 January 1912, Sneed Habeas Corpus Transcript. 249.

87   AGB Jr. to LSS, 15 January 1912, ibid., 253.

88   Letter of AGB Jr. to LSS, 20 January 1912, ibid., 257.

89   See *Dallas Morning News*, 18 February 1912, photocopy in Pool Collection, for Henry Boyce's description of Al's personality as compared with Beal's: "I knew my brother was cool and nervy and Sneed was excitable and nervous." See also the testimony of Joe Barr in Sneed Habeas Corpus Transcript, 140-149, describing his encounters with Al and Lucien Hughes, wherein Al's manner sounds cool and restrained.

90   LSS to AGB Jr., 2 February 1912, Boyce Collection. I have left Lena's punctuation and spelling as they appear in the letters.

91   LSS to AGB Jr., 2 March 1912, ibid.

92   LSS to AGB Jr., 31 March 1912; LSS to AGB Jr., 23 April 1912, ibid.

93   LSS to AGB Jr., 18 May 1912, ibid.

94   Sneed Habeas Corpus Transcript, 223.

95   Ibid., 226 and 229.

96   *Manitoba Free Press*, 1 or 2 January 1912, date uncertain.

97   *Fort Worth Star-Telegram*, 27 December 1912.

98   A letter Lena wrote on 27 March 1912 refers to a show she and Al had seen in Chicago. LSS to AGB Jr., 22 March 1912, Boyce Collection. Hotel registers from the Hotel Rome in Omaha and from the Regent Hotel in Winnipeg, where the couple registered as Mr. and Mrs. A. J. Brooks, were used as evidence to document their movements. *Fort Worth Star-Telegram*, 30 January 1912.

99 *Manitoba Free Press*, 27 December 1911.

100 The *Free Press* seems frequently to have published inaccurate "background" information on the story. It quoted Al at length on occasion, although he says in one of his letters to Lena that he talked to no one, and that the "interviews" are false. AGB Jr. to LSS, 13 January 1912, Sneed Habeas Corpus Transcript, 249. The paper also reported that Al had abducted Lena by driving his motor car onto the grounds at Arlington Heights and having her passed out the window to him, an apparent amalgam of the circumstances of the elopement and Beal's behavior with the nurse (date uncertain, probably 1 January 1912). *The Free Press*, 29 December 1911 also reported that Beal had brought his two daughters with him to Winnipeg, daughters who mysteriously turned into sons awaiting Lena in Minneapolis, ibid., 3 January 1912. Lena is quoted as saying that this "was a case of love at first sight, and a few weeks after their first meeting they decided to elope." ibid., 27 December 1911. Despite these inaccuracies, I have generally assumed that with regard to the legal maneuvering that took place in Canada, the paper is the most accurate source, particularly if combined with Beal's testimony.

101 Sneed Habeas Corpus Transcript, 230.

102 Ibid, 231-232.

103 For the account of what occurred in Canada, I have synopsized accounts from the following sources; *Fort Worth Star-Telegram*, 27, 29, 30, 31 December 1911 and 2 January 1912;

Amarillo Daily News, 31 December 1911 and 1 January 1912; *Manitoba Free Press*, 27, 28, 29, 31 December 1911 and 1, 3, 4, 10, 13, 15 January 1912; letter from AGB Jr. to LSS, 13 January 1912, Sneed Habeas Corpus Transcript, 249; the letters of LSS to AGB Jr. undated, written in Canada between 31 December 1911 and 2 January 1912; the LSS telegram to Henry Boyce of 28 December 1911; the LSS letter to Henry Boyce of 5 January 1912 and the LSS letter to AGB Jr. of 8 January 1912 (all LSS correspondence from the Boyce Collection); as well as Beal's own testimony in his habeas corpus hearing, and the accounts of other persons' testimony in the *Star-Telegram*. The legal maneuvering that took place throughout this period is complex and differently reported, depending on the newspaper. The *Free Press* consistently reports that Al was indicted for grand larceny in Fort Worth, which I believe to be incorrect because the *Star-Telegram* reports an indictment for abduction only. In the case of events in Canada, I have assumed the *Free Press* to be the more accurate source, though that paper is frequently inaccurate about personal details and was not above making up quotes for the participants, at least judging from Al's 13 January 1912 letter in which he wrote that all the "interviews" with him that have been published were false, and that he has not spoken to the papers at all. See AGB Jr. to LSS, 13 January 1912.

104 *Fort Worth Star-Telegram*, 21 February 1912, report of testimony of Sheriff W.M. Rea.

Sheriff Rea stated that his telegram was based on information provided to him by Will Atwell. At the time of the telegram, Al had not been indicted for larceny in Fort Worth.

105 *Manitoba Free Press*, date uncertain, probably 2 January 1912. Note that the *Star-Telegram* states the Texas indictment against Al was for abduction only, but later *Star-Telegram* reports seem to imply that rape charges were included in the charges of abduction.

106 LSS to AGB Jr., date uncertain, Boyce Collection, sometime after 30 December 1911 when Beal arrived in Winnipeg and before 2 January 1912 when Lena was deported, most probably 31 December, as Lena says Beal was "here tonight and last night also."

107 Ibid.

108 Letter of LSS to Henry Boyce, 5 January 1912, Boyce Collection; *Manitoba Free Press*, 3 January 1912.

109 *Manitoba Free Press*, 10 January 1912.

110 LSS to Henry Boyce, 5 January 1912, Boyce Collection.

111 *Manitoba Free Press*, 15 January 1912. This paper also seems to have made up interviews with Al, whom they quoted quite freely, but who insisted "The papers . . . have published what purported to be interviews with me, but I have talked to no one." AGB Jr. to LSS, 15 January 1912, Sneed Habeas Corpus Transcript, 253.

112 *Winnipeg Saturday*, date uncertain, Boyce Collection, possibly 6 January 1912, the first

Saturday after Lena's deportation. Note that this idea that Lena has been forced to accept being deported floated through the Canadian newspaper accounts. The Free Press reported rumors of a deal Lena had made to return to Beal "on the understanding that she would not be again incarcerated in the sanitarium, and that she would be allowed to give her testimony at the [abduction] trial of Boyce." *Manitoba Free Press*, 3 January 1912. Lena herself, in one of her undated notes to Al composed while she was in Canada, wrote, "Oh, Albert I just feel like we won't be together again for precious if we are not deported, I am going back to Texas to save you—from these awful charges." Boyce Collection, In her first letter to Henry Boyce, however, Lena writes, "I was deported from Canada Tuesday." LSS to Henry Boyce, 6 January 1912, Boyce Collection.

113 *Winnipeg Saturday*, date uncertain, possibly 6 January 1912, Boyce Collection.

114 *Fort Worth Star-Telegram*, 31 December 1911.

115 Ibid.

116 LSS to Henry Boyce, 10 January 1912; LSS to AGB Jr., January 1912, Boyce Collection.

117 LSS to AGB Jr., 8 January 1912, Boyce Collection.

118 AGB Jr. to LSS, 13 January 1912, Sneed Habeas Corpus Transcript, 249.

119 John Beal Sneed testimony, Habeas Corpus Transcript, 236.

120 AGB Jr. to LSS, 13 January 1912, Sneed Habeas Corpus Transcript, 250.

121 Sneed Habeas Corpus Transcript, 235.

122 Telegram from LSS to Henry Boyce, 12 January 1912, Boyce Collection.

123 LSS to AGB Jr., undated notes written in Canada between 31 December 1911 and 2 January 1912, Boyce Collection.

124 *Fort Worth Star-Telegram*, 2 February 1912, report of testimony of John Pace.

125 Sneed Habeas Corpus Transcript. 238.

126 *Fort Worth Star-Telegram*, 16 February 1912, letter quoted in full in account of Henry Boyce's testimony.

127 *Fort Worth Star-Telegram*, 17 February 1912.

128 Ibid.

129 *Fort Worth Star-Telegram*, 2 February 1912, report of testimony of W. H. Atwell.

130 In later trials, Beal testified that the Colonel was rising when he shot him, and had made the remark, "Here comes the (blank) now." Although there is a great deal of confusing testimony from eyewitnesses, the predominant opinion seems to be that the Colonel was seated when Beal began shooting and said nothing prior to the shots. Neither witness who testified to the epithet was considered reliable; the second was charged with perjury. One J. D. Covey, who rode in the ambulance with the Colonel to the hospital, said the Colonel stated that no words were exchanged prior to the shooting. *Fort Worth*

Star-Telegram, 15 February 1912.

131   Account of the circumstances leading up to the killing and the killing itself are taken from testimony of Beal Sneed Habeas Corpus Transcript, 243-246; *Fort Worth Star-Telegram*, account of W. H. Atwell testimony, 2 February 1912; as well as the reports of various witnesses given in the *Star-Telegram* throughout the trials. It is worth noting that the account of the supper at Joseph's is drawn from Atwell's, Bowman's, and Beal's testimony, none of whom were disinterested witnesses. The fact that the Colonel made, at one time or another, insulting remarks about Lena seems indisputable because so many witnesses heard them in Amarillo. Whether he was indiscreet enough to make them to Will Atwell is more questionable.

132   AGB Jr. to LSS, 13 January 1912, Sneed Habeas Corpus Transcript, 251-252.

133   LSS to AGB Jr., 2 February 1912, Boyce Collection.

134   In a letter to Lena written on January 18, Al says, "My desire and impulse was to return, but have received telegrams asking me to stay in Canada, and everyone here has told me my presence there would only aggravate the situation and weaken the prosecution. That I would be arrested upon crossing the line, and it would only mean more trouble," AGB Jr. to LSS, 18 January 1912, Sneed Habeas Corpus Transcript, 255.

135   *Manitoba Free Press*, 18 or 19 January

1912.

136 *Fort Worth Star-Telegram*, 19 January 1912.

137 This practice, which seems startling today, is in fact still legal, though rarely used. Judge John Forbis, phone interview with the author, Memphis, Texas, February, 1997.

138 *Fort Worth Star-Telegram*, 19 January 1912.

139 Ibid. This evidence of Allison's is one of the reasons a miscarriage at the sanitarium seems unlikely, since Lena would hardly have been causing such trouble if she had been physically unwell.

140 Ibid., 20 January 1912.

141 Ibid. It seems apparent, both from Lena's reference to what came out in the hearing that could not be printed in the papers, and from the curiously curtailed feel of the *Star-Telegram* account of Lena's testimony (which, in contrast to the paper's usual practice, uses no direct quotes), that things are missing. This is almost certainly due to the nature of the testimony, and perhaps a certain sense of chivalry on the part of the *Star-Telegram*'s reporter.

142 LSS to AGB. Jr., 2 February 1912, Boyce Collection. Lena means she drew on Al's bank account in Dalhart.

143 AGB Jr. to LSS. 20 January 1912, Sneed Habeas Corpus Transcript, see also endnote 148. Calomel is mercury chloride and was used as general tonic at the time, despite being poisonous. Lattimore's object in the questioning is to show that the treatment was insignificant in comparison to the alleged degree of disease.

144   LSS to AGB. Jr., 7 February 1912. Boyce Collection.

145   LSS to AGB. Jr., 9 March 1912, ibid.

146   LSS to AGB. Jr., 2 March 1912. ibid.

147   LSS to AGB Jr., 8 March 1912, ibid.

148   By 9 February 1912, Lena's letters were being mailed from Lake Charles. Her letter of 2 February to Al bemoans the fact that she has not heard one word from him since she left Canada. The letters Al wrote to her which were used as exhibits in the habeas corpus hearing were delivered to Clayton, New Mexico, after she had been confined to the sanitarium. Addressed on the outer envelope to John Pace, her brother-in-law whom she initially believed was on her side, these letters were held by the Clayton postmaster until Pace and Tom Snyder returned to Clayton after Beal's first trial. The defense claimed the postmaster delivered the letters to Snyder. This seems unlikely as they were addressed to Pace, but the defense did not want to make an issue of Pace's apparent change of loyalties. Lena initially told Al that Pace "acted the scamp" (LSS to AGB Jr.. 2 February 1912. Boyce Collection), but later wrote that she had heard that Beal told Pace that if he supported Lena, Beal would "blow his head off" (LSS to AGB Jr., 9 February 1912, Boyce Collection). One does not find the latter possibility out of the question.

149 *Fort Worth Star-Telegram*, 24 January 1912.

150 Ibid., 24-31 January 1912.

151 Selcer, *Hell's Half Acre*, I60-I61.

152 *Fort Worth Star-Telegram*, 31 January 1912.

153 Ibid., 4 February 1912.

154 The defense put two witnesses on the stand in Beal's two trials for killing the Colonel, both of whom testified that when Beal entered the lobby of the Metropolitan after supper on 13 January, the Colonel said, "There goes the (blank) now." Beal himself testified that he heard the epithet upon entering the lobby. *Fort Worth Star-Telegram*, 15 February 1912. E. D. Powers testified in the first trial, W. A. Weaver testified in the second. Powers' testimony and general veracity was questioned by the prosecution: On the night following his testimony, he got into a fist fight with a friend of the Boyces. Weaver was impeached and charged with perjury—evidence being developed that he could not have been in the lobby at the time he said he was. *Fort Worth Star-Telegram*, 18 January 1912 and 25 November 1912. The preponderance of disinterested testimony seems to indicate the Colonel did not rise from his chair until after Beal began firing and that no words were exchanged between the two. See report of testimony of John W. Covey, *Fort Worth Star-Telegram*. 15 February 1912.

One of the lingering questions about the murder is whether it was premeditated; Beal,

Atwell, and Bowman concurred that Beal had
returned to the hotel to use the toilet. As the
prosecution pointed out, however, Atwell had
earlier stated Beal returned for his grip; none of
these witnesses were disinterested; and a toilet
was available at Joseph's. On the other hand,
there seems little doubt that the Colonel was
planning to leave town that evening, so that if
Beal had decided at dinner to kill him, he could
hardly have been certain he would still be sitting
in the hotel lobby. Perhaps he entered the lobby
with a kind of boiling rage to confront the
Colonel if he was still there and, on seeing him,
simply opened fire, without ever having thought
the action completely through. In all Beal's
other actions throughout the affair, deliberation
to the point of obsessiveness seems clear: Here
was a man who thoroughly understood how
to "work" the legal system and how to present
a sympathetic face to jurors. In the murder of
the Colonel only does he seem to have lost his
head, and he could hardly have been certain of
acquittal. Had he been convicted, Lena would
surely have been able to procure a divorce.

155 LSS to AGB Jr., 2 February 1912, Boyce
Collection.

156 I have synopsized what I believe were
the primary successful defense arguments. Beal's
attorneys had a certain scatter-shot approach to
his defense, at times pleading, as will be seen,
self-defense and temporary insanity.

157 AGB. Jr. to LSS. 13 January 1912, Sneed

Habeas Corpus Transcript, 251. Al wrote, "I wrote Ma and Pa a day or so after you left telling them how you and I loved each other, and how you had suffered and gone through Hell itself for me, and I don't think she [Mrs. Boyce] will feel hard towards you or talk hard about you anymore but will understand and love you. It hurts me worse than it does you, Darling. Anyone that knows you or comes in contact with you knows you to be the purest and best of women [sic] you have few equals and no superiors and everyone loves and respects you." Colonel Boyce's "stand hitched" letter probably followed receipt of the letter to which Al refers, which must have been written on 1 or 2 January 1912. Needless to say, Al was overly optimistic about his mother's future opinion of Lena.

158 *Dallas Morning News*, 20 February 1912. Photocopy from Pool Collection.

159 For descriptions of Colonel Boyce's personality, as well as the history of his employment at the XIT, I have relied on Haley, *XIT Ranch*, Nordyke, *Cattle Empire*, and Joe B. Frantz and Cordia Sloan Duke, *6000 Miles of Fence, Life on the XIT Ranch of Texas* (Austin: University of Texas Press, 1961, 1992).

160 Haley, *XIT Ranch*, 150.

161 *Fort Worth Star-Telegram*, 9 and 10 February 1912, report of testimony of L.O. Thompson. J. H. Slade, and Ray Wheatley. The impression one has from these accounts is that the Colonel, used to talking "men's talk" to men, had misjudged the gravity of the situation and indulged in a lifelong habit of blunt speech. Arch Sneed, an XIT cowboy (no direct relation), characterized the Colonel as having "a kind of fatherly way about him with his men and (as being) rough in his language in giving advice." See Duke and Frantz, *6000 Miles of Fence*, 214. Two days before the Colonel was killed, Henry Boyce wired his father, "Don't talk much." See *Fort Worth Star-Telegram*, 9 February 1912. One imagines Henry recognized the dangers of overly frank speech, in part from Lena's letters about her father's reaction to the *Star-Telegram* interviews of 31 December 1911. Perhaps the Colonel was also secretly embarrassed and bewildered by the situation and sought to cover his confusion by an over-hearty manner and injudicious comments. Witnesses are equally convincing in their reports that the Colonel repeatedly expressed disapproval of Al's behavior in the weeks following the elopement. Wheatley testified that the Colonel said, in a meeting the two had about a shipment of cattle feed, that "he [the Colonel] didn't know what was the matter with Albert, that he could do nothing with him. . . . [T]hat the affair had been going on some time, and that he had done everything he could to break it off. . . . [I]t was distressing his wife to death. He had even offered to sell out everything and divide with Albert, and go anywhere he said, if he would only discontinue the practice." See *Fort Worth Star-Telegram*, 10 February 1912.

162   Haley. *XIT Ranch*. 214-215. In 1927, Haley interviewed William Boyce, the Colonel's oldest son. William described the situation: "There was a good deal of feeling over the case that came up in which the company was almost placed in the hands of receivers. . . . Babcock's allegation was that the Farwells, who were the largest stockholders, were using the ranch to their personal interests and to the detriment of the minority stockholders. They appointed a receiver without any notice to the company at all. This was done through Judge H. H. Wallace. ...W. H. Fuqua and J. V. Goode, who was superintendent of the Fort Worth & Denver railroad, were appointed receivers. Judge Wallace was a meddlesome sort of fellow, disliked Boyce, my father, and was friendly to Fuqua and Goode. He appointed the receivers without notifying the defendants."

'They did not know that the giving of the supersedes bonds suspended the right of the receivers taking charge of the property. . . . Judge Wallace set [bond] at $25,000. After giving the bond and the decision was rendered in the courts, it was like exploding a bombshell with Fuqua and Goode. Of course, they expected to make a great deal of money off of it. It has always been quite a sore spot with Fuqua. It made an enemy of him and my father. My father was always a very positive man." See William Boyce. Interview with J. Evetts Haley, Amarillo, Texas, 28 June 1927, Nita Stewart Haley Memorial

Library, Midland, Texas.

163 *Fort Worth Star-Telegram*, 9 February 1912, letter quoted in full.

164 *Dallas Morning News*, 15 February 1912.

165 *Fort Worth Star-Telegram*, 9 February 1912.

166 Ibid., 23 January 1912.

167 Ibid., 7 February 1912.

168 LSS to AGB Jr., 2 February 1912, Boyce Collection.

169 *Fort Worth Star-Telegram*, 19 February 1912.

170 Ibid.

171 Ibid.

172 Ibid.

173 *Dallas Morning News*, 20 February 1912.

174 *Fort Worth Star-Telegram,* 19 February 1912.

175 *Dallas Morning News*, 20 February 1912.

176 *Fort Worth Star-Telegram*, 3 February 1912.

177 Ibid., 19 February 1912.

178 Ibid., 7 February 1912.

179 LSS to AGB Jr., 9 February 1912, Boyce Collection.

180 Beal claimed that Lena attempted to prevent him from using their telephone to wire her father to come from Clayton and that he "picked her up and took her in the bedroom and laid her on the bed." Sneed Habeas Corpus Transcript, 207. Mrs. Boyce testified that Tom Snyder told her essentially the same story when she asked him about the bruises. *Fort Worth Star-Telegram*, 19 February 1912.

181 *Fort Worth Star-Telegram*, 19 February 1912.

182 T. S. Snyder, report of cross-examination in ibid., 7 February 1912; Eula Bowman, report of testimony in ibid., 21 February 1912. There was an intriguing exchange between Eula and McLean wherein—after Eula testified that there were no bruises or scratches on Lena's neck—McLean asked her, "[Did Mrs. Sneed say] anything about a suspender clasp?" "I don't remember," was Eula's reply.

183 Sneed Habeas Corpus Transcript, 207.

184 *Fort Worth Star-Telegram*, 19 February 1912, Tom Snyder quoted by Annie Boyce.

185 *Manitoba Free Press*, 15 January 1912. One quotes any of this kind of information from the *Free Press* with trepidation, as the paper was clearly not above inventing "color" or quotes if necessary. However, the description of Lena's opinion accords closely enough with the impression formed from reading her letters to Al to give it some credence.

186 LSS to AGB Jr., 18 May 1912, Boyce Collection. Letter details a conversation with her sister Eula wherein Eula informs her she believes Beal intends to kill Lena. Lena seems genuinely afraid of Beal and particularly afraid of what Beal might do to Al. On the other hand, at times one has the impression that she was equally afraid that Al might leave her and it is possible she exaggerated her danger in order to play on Al's chivalrous impulses.

187   LSS to AGB Jr, n.d., letter written in Canada, Boyce Collection.

188   LSS to AGB Jr, 23 April 1912, Boyce Collection.

189   This general impression is formed from Lena's account of Beal's various maneuvers during the months following the Colonel's death. These included intercepting Lena's mail from Al; pursuing federal white slavery charges against Al; persuading Lena to sign a release for the rings she had left with Murray in Canada and then refusing to send them to her; persuading her to sign off on a sale of the Amarillo property—which she owned in part—on the assurance that she would receive the interest from it, and then not sending her any money; possibly refusing to allow the children to write her, or preventing them from receiving gifts and letters she sent to them; as well as possibly hiring people to watch her. Both Beal and Lena were intelligent enough to realize that his defense at the trial made it imperative that he appear to be primarily interested in her welfare. One comes away, however, with the sense of a man whose obsession with vanquishing his foes never ceased and whose mind was ever active and agile in finding new ways to increase the odds in his favor. My own family lore indicates that Beal was the sort who could eventually talk almost anyone into anything, simply because whomever he was trying to persuade just got tired of listening to him.

190 Pool Collection, letters dating from 17 March 1913 to 28 November 1925. These letters are almost exclusively—indeed, one might say, obsessively—engaged with business matters. Loan percentages, tenant leases, and cotton and cattle conditions and prices comprise the bulk of most of them. Considering that the first letter, to Joe Sneed. Jr., is written not much more than two weeks after Beal's final acquittal, its limits in terms of subject matter are notable.

191 *Fort Worth Star-Telegram*, 16 February 1912.

192 Ibid., 9 February 1912.

193 Ibid., 19 February 1912.

194 Ibid., 9 and 10 February 1912.

195 Ibid., 19 February 1912, report of testimony of Mrs. Boyce.

196 Ibid., 9 February 1912. This telegram is reported as dated 23 December 1912, but I believe this is an error; the date should possibly be the 28 December 1912.

197 Ibid., 15 February 1912.

198 Ibid., 14 February 1912.

199 Ibid.

200 LSS to AGB Jr. 2 February 1912, Boyce Collection.

201 *Fort Worth Star-Telegram*, 9 February 1912. The practice of bringing children to court, where their presence might force the jury to consider the effect of its verdict on the defendant's family, was evidently considered entirely acceptable at the time, as it would not be today. One can imagine, for example, only negative effects if O.J. Simpson had brought his children to court.

202 Ibid., 22 February 1912.

203 Ibid., 23 February 1912.

204 *Dallas Morning News*, 23 February 1912.

205 *Fort Worth Star-Telegram*, 29 February 1912.

206 Ibid., 3 March 1912.

207 Ibid., 14 March 1912.

208 Ibid., 29 February 1912.

209 Ibid., 31 January 1912.

210 Ibid., 31 January 1912 through 3 February 1912.

211 Ibid., 20 February 1912.

212 Ibid., 17 February 1912.

213 Ibid., 3 March 1912.

214 LSS to AGB Jr., 8 March 1912, Boyce Collection.

215 LSS to AGB Jr., 21 March 1912, Boyce Collection. My father has always said that the death was convenient for Beal in another way as well: J.T. Sneed Sr. had told his son that he would help him get through the legal actions resulting from the Colonel's murder but that in return he expected Beal to leave Lena, and if he did not, his father planned to cut him off.

216 *Fort Worth Star-Telegram*, 6 February 1912. The description of smoking in the courtroom is interesting not only because it highlights a difference between that time and this one, but also because Al was described as a "cigarette fiend." Judging from Barry's account and a later *Star-Telegram* report of courtroom smoking, one concludes that if Al was addicted to smoking, he had plenty of company. On 17 November 1912, during the second trial for the killing of the Colonel, the *Star-Telegram* reported on Judge Swayne's difficulty in enforcing his ban on smoking. Beal was reported chewing on a cigar—though Kitty Barry earlier had claimed the female presence deprived him of his "friendly brown pipe;" Sheriff Rea was smoking a cigar; the newspaper man directly beneath the judge had a foul-smelling pipe which the reporter believed to be the source of Swayne's continuing irritation on the subject; and Bill McLean was, like Al, smoking cigarettes. Perhaps, despite the fact that the defense counsel indulged in them, cigarettes conveyed a "faster" impression than did pipes or cigars.

217 Ibid., 17 November 1912.

218 Ibid.

219 Ibid., 24 February 1912.

220 LSS to AGB Jr., 8 March 1912, Boyce Collection.

221 *Fort Worth Star-Telegram*, 14 January 1912.

222 Ibid.

223 Ibid.

224 LSS to AGB Jr., 8 March 1912, Boyce Collection.

225 Ibid.

226 LSS to AGB Jr., 9 March 1912, ibid.

227 LSS to AGB Jr., 10 March 1912, ibid.

228 Ibid. As previously mentioned, the allusions to pregnancy or venereal disease are fairly clear and Lena seems to have had no problem understanding what was meant by them. "Nymphomania" is an old enough term to have been in at least specialized use at the time; it relates to female sexual excess; and it would probably not have been a word a respectable woman would ever have heard. For those reasons I suggest it as the idea behind the report Lena could not bring herself to relate to Al, though she wrote she might find the courage to tell him when she saw him.

229 LSS to AGB Jr., 12 March 1912, Boyce Collection.

230 LSS to AGB Jr., 10 March 1912. Ibid.

231 John Blanton testimony, Sneed Habeas Corpus Transcript. 155.

232 LSS to Pearl Snyder, 17 April 1912, Boyce Collection. This letter gives the details of the transaction by which Beal induced Lena to sign the deed to the house.

233 Blanton testimony, Sneed Habeas Corpus Transcript. 176-177.

234 LSS to AGB Jr., 18 March 1912, Boyce Collection.

235 Billie Steele, Sneed Habeas Corpus Transcript, 119.

236 Ibid. Lena reported she had chosen a long

route to California because it was the cheapest.

237 Ibid.

238 LSS to AGB Jr., 24 March 1912, Boyce Collection.

239 LSS to AGB Jr., 18 March 1912, ibid.

240 The business of the federal indictment is confusing. Lena wrote on 29 March 1912 that the grand jury had not returned an indictment. Henry Boyce, however, was troubled throughout the spring by reports that an indictment had been filed, at least judging from Lena's letters to Al. LSS to AGB Jr., 29 and 31 March 1912 and 21 May 1912, Boyce Collection. In the last, she rejoices that Atwell will "be forced to dismiss this indictment and I know it will sure make him sore."

241 LSS to T. J. Murray, 17 April 1912, Boyce Collection.

242 LSS to Pearl Snyder, 17 April 1912, ibid., reporting that Nell writes Billie "every time I spit."

243 LSS to T. J. Murray, 17 April 1912, ibid.

244 LSS to AGB Jr.. 2 March 1912 and 6 April 1912, ibid. These two letters emphasize her illnesses, but a number of others allude to it. One has the impression that she was unwell most of the time after she left Canada.

245 LSS to AGB Jr., 6 April 1912, ibid.

246 LSS to T. J. Murray and LSS to Pearl Snyder, 17 April 1912, ibid.

247 LSS to unknown man, probably Al's bodyguard; probably hand delivered, not postmarked or addressed, dated 20 April 1912, ibid.

248 This account is based on notes and letters from LSS to AGB. Jr., written between 20 and 23 April 1912, ibid.

249 Ibid.

250 Hamlin, *The Flamboyant Judge*, 96.

251 LSS to AGB Jr., 23 April 1912 through 21 May 1912, Boyce Collection. The Haley footnote suggests Al returned to Texas and then went back to California, but judging from trial accounts of his movements in Texas, this does not seem to have been the case. In an interview with the author in Alamo, California, in November of 1994. Gary Radder, Ira Aten's grandson, who still owns the ranch in El Centro, was unable to verify Aten's reported comment to Haley.

252 LSS to AGB. Jr., 4 May 1912, Boyce Collection.

253 LSS to AGB. Jr., IH May 1912 and 5 May 1912, ibid.

254 LSS to AGB Jr., 4 May 1912, ibid.

255 LSS to AGB Jr., 18 May 1912. ibid.

256 Ibid.

257 LSS to AGB Jr.. 21 May 1912, ibid.

258 Blanton testimony, Sneed Habeas Corpus Transcript, 177-180.

259 Ibid., 180-181.

260 Billie Steele testimony. ibid, 119-120.

261 Ibid, 121.

262 Blanton testimony, ibid., 158. Blanton's testimony is somewhat confusing, but on the subject of Beal's and Lena's movements is generally supported by Billie Steele's testimony, ibid., 121.

263 Mrs. L. A. Rogers testimony, ibid. 86.

264 LSS to AGB Jr, 10 August 1912. Boyce Collection.

265 *Fort Worth Star-Telegram*, 21 September 1912.

266 Blanton testimony, Sneed Habeas Corpus Transcript. 157.

267 Lynn Boyce testimony, ibid., 108.

268 Blanton testimony, ibid., 189.

269 *Fort Worth Star-Telegram*, 18 January 1913.

270 Ibid., 26 September 1912.

271 Blanton testimony, Sneed Habeas Corpus Transcript, 188.

272 Ibid., 183-184.

273 Mrs. L. A. Rogers testimony, ibid., 87-92.

274 Mrs. L. A. Rogers testified that Lena destroyed Al's letters to her, ibid., 88; Pearl writes that she burned Al's letter, ibid. Pearl Snyder Perkins to LSS, 19 July 1912, 261, ibid; and Lena's last surviving letter to Al is marked on the top "Please destroy this." One imagines that Al, in a romantic gesture, did not destroy her last letter until he received her next one. As Lena and Beal left the Reiger Avenue house on 13 August, Al may never have received another letter from Lena.

275 Mrs. L. A. Rogers testimony, ibid., 89.

276 LSS to AGB Jr, 10 August 1912, Boyce

Collection.

277 *Fort Worth Star-Telegram*, 16 September 1912.

278 Pearl Snyder Perkins to LSS, 19 July 1912, Sneed Habeas Corpus Transcript, 261; Billie Steele testimony, ibid., 121.

279 Mrs. L. A. Rogers testimony, ibid., 93.

280 AGB Jr. to Pearl Snyder Perkins, 14 August 1912, ibid., 250.

281 Mrs. L. A. Rogers testimony, ibid., 99.

282 Ibid., 101-102.

283 LSS to AGB Jr., 23 April 1912, Boyce Collection.

284 LSS to AGB Jr., three undated letters probably written between 20 April and 23 April 1912, Boyce Collection.

285 Ibid., third of the undated notes.

286 Throughout her letters, Lena refers to her desire for a pregnancy and wonders when might be an appropriate time to consider one. This indicates that the lovers had at least a rudimentary notion of birth control, so that the pregnancy in August must be regarded as choice rather than accident.

287 LSS to AGB Jr., 10 August 1912, Boyce Collection. Lena remarks that Blanton, whom at this point she believed to be an ally, told her he thought Beal had headed for Amarillo, then writes: "Of course if you stay on in Amarillo—I believe Beal will finally come."

288 Mrs. L. A. Rogers testimony, Sneed Habeas Corpus Transcript, 95.

289 LSS to AGB Jr., 10 August 1912, Boyce Collection.

290 LSS to AGB Jr., undated note written in Canada, probably between 28 December 1911 and 2 January 1912, Boyce Collection.

291 Ibid. While I have provisionally placed this note before the previous one, it could easily have followed it.

292 LSS to AGB Jr., 6 April 1912, ibid.

293 *Fort Worth Star-Telegram*, 17 February 1912.

294 Pearl Snyder Perkins to LSS, 17 July 1912, Sneed Habeas Corpus Transcript, 261.

295 *Fort Worth Star-Telegram*, 18 September 1912.

296 Blanton testimony, Sneed Habeas Corpus Transcript, 160; Joe Barr testimony, ibid., 140.

297 Barr testimony, ibid., 140.

298 Blanton testimony, ibid., 161-162.

299 Report of testimony of John Beal Sneed, quoted in *Fort Worth Star-Telegram*, 20 February 1913.

300 Blanton testimony, Sneed Habeas Corpus Transcript, 164.

301 Testimony of Sam Bass, reported in *Fort Worth Star-Telegram*, 15 February 1913.

302 Testimony of Sam Bass, ibid., 21 February 1913.

303 Testimony of Beech Epting, ibid., 20 February 1913.

304 Ibid., January 1913.

305 Testimony of J. H. Avery, ibid., 21 February 1913.

306 Mrs. T. F. McKibben testimony, Sneed Habeas Corpus Transcript, 61-62.

307 O. K. Gilvin testimony, ibid.. 66-67. Gilvin, a self-styled "real estate agent," rented the "death cottage" to Beech Epting for Beal.

308 Lynn Boyce testimony, ibid., 108-109.

309 W. M. Burwell testimony, ibid., 14-15. Burwell was Potter County sheriff and a state witness.

310 Lynn Boyce testimony, ibid.. 110.

311 Ibid., 111.

312 E. E. Robinson testimony, ibid., 25-26.

313 Ibid., 27.

314 Earl Jackson testimony, ibid., 34.

315 E. E. Robinson, recall testimony, ibid., 31.

316 Earl Jackson testimony, ibid., 34.

317 E. E. Robinson, recall testimony, ibid., 31.

318 Earl Jackson testimony, ibid., 37-39. Jackson's testimony is delightful and has about it the ring of youth and truth.

319 E. E. Robinson testimony, ibid., 28.

320 John F. Speed testimony, ibid., 191.

321 C.J. Collier testimony, ibid., 193. Presumably. Collier referred to LaGrange. Texas.

322 Ibid., 194.

323 A.F. Lumpkin testimony, ibid., 22-24.

324 Jim T. Green testimony, ibid., 59.

325 Roxana Robinson. *Georgia O'Keeffe, A*

Life (New York: Harper & Row. An Edward Burlingame Book. 1989). 88-89; Lisle Laurie, *Portrait of an Artist, A Biography of Georgia O'Keeffe* (New York: Seaview Books. 1980), 51-52.

326 Mrs. Maria (J.M.) Kindred testimony, Sneed Habeas Corpus Transcript, 47.

327 *Fort Worth Star-Telegram*, 16 September 1912.

328 Ibid., 21 September 1912.

329 Ibid., 28 September 1912.

330 Ibid., 30 October 1912.

331 Ibid., 11 November 1912.

332 Ibid., 9 November 1912.

333 Ibid., 13 November 1912.

334 Ibid., 15 November 1912.

335 Ibid., 16 November 1912.

336 Ibid., 17 November 1912.

337 Ibid., 15 November 1912.

338 Ibid., 21 and 22 November 1912.

339 Ibid., 22 November 1912.

340 Ibid., 21 November 1912.

341 Ibid., 25 November 1912. The *Star-Telegram* printed the epithet as shown.

342 Ibid., 21 November 1912.

343 Ibid., 19 November 1912.

344 Ibid., 25 November 1912.

345 Ibid., 2 December 1912.

346 Ibid., 3 December 1912.

347 Ibid., 3 December 1912.

348 *Amarillo Daily News*, 4 December 1912.

349 *Fort Worth Star-Telegram*, 3 December 1912.

350 Ibid.

351 Ibid., 6 January 1913.

352 Ibid., 8 January 1913.

353 Ibid., 17 January 1913.

354 Ibid., 12 January 1913.

355 Ibid.

356 Ibid., 16 January 1913.

357 Ibid., 20 January 1913.

358 Ibid., 15 January 1913.

359 Ibid., 19 January 1913.

360 Ibid., 21 January 1913.

361 Ibid.

362 Ibid., 23 January 1913.

363 Ibid., 13 February 1913.

364 Ibid.

365 Ibid., 14 February 1913.

366 Ibid., 20 and 21 February 1913.

367 Ibid., 21 February 1913.

368 Ibid., 19 February 1913.

369 Ibid. There was obviously some confusion, probably on the reporter's part, about when this confinement occurred. What was described is a conflation of the confinement at Arlington Heights after Lena's return from Canada and the confinement at Johnson's after her return from California.

370 Ibid., 19 February 1913.

371 Ibid., 14 February 1913.

372 Joe Barr testimony, Sneed Habeas Corpus Transcript, 144-145.

373 Ibid., 145.

374 Ibid., 148.

375   W. J. Blair testimony, ibid., 151. Blair was a Fort Worth real estate agent and a former director of the Boyce bank in Dalhart. He testified, reluctantly, as a defense witness.

376   LSS to AGB Jr., 20 February 1912, Boyce Collection.

377   LSS to AGB Jr., 2 March 1912, ibid.

378   LSS to AGB. Jr., 27 March 1912, ibid.

379   *Fort Worth Star-Telegram*, 22 February 1913.

380   Ibid., 19 February 1913.

381   Earl McFarland to John Beal Sneed, registered letter, 24 June 1912, Boyce Collection. One can only surmise that Lena found this letter and gave it to Al, since how it ended up in his possession is otherwise inexplicable.

382   *Fort Worth Star-Telegram*, 8 October 1922.

383   Ibid., 22 February 1913.

384   Ibid., 24 February 1913.

385   Ibid., 22 February 1913.

386   Ibid., 24 February 1913.

387   Ibid., 25 February 1913.

388   Account taken from *Paducah Post* files, reprinted in Carmen Taylor Bennet, *Our Roots Grow Deep, A History of Cottle County* (Floydada, Texas: Blanco Offset Printing, Inc. 1970) and from Michael Hughes "Old West Tales— Feudin' fussin', fightin' part of Paducah history," *Amarillo Daily News*, 28 December 1993; and from timeline created by Joseph H. Pool, Pool Collection.

389   Account formed from *Fort Worth Star-*

Telegram, 8 October 1922 (handwritten copy from Pool Collection); a Certified Copy of Indictment, and Judgement and sentence No. 785—Criminal, United States District Court, Northern District of Texas at Abilene, The United States against John Beall [sic] Sneed, et al (xerox copy from Pool Collection); correspondence of B. Sneed with his brother, J. T. Sneed, in particular the letters of 9 June 1924, 18 June 1924 and 21 June 1924. The June 21 letter includes a message from Senator Morris Shepard: "President notified me through Attorney General about noon today that he could not grant pardon at this time. Strongly intimated that after service of sentence for about thirty days pardon would be favorably considered on renewal of application. Both President and Attorney General stated that this decision was final and further consideration could not be granted at this time." Xerox copies from Pool Collection.

390 *Dallas Morning News*, 23 April 1960.

391 Ibid., 7 March 1966.

392 Dr. Charies A. Perkins, Lake Charles, Louisiana, telephone interview with author, August 1996.

393 *Amarillo Daily News*, 26 February 1913.

394 Ibid., 18 September 1912.

395 Sonnischen, *I'll Die Before I'll Run*, 10.

396 Alward White, telephone interview with the author. Amarillo, Texas, May 1995.

Clara Sneed was born in Texas and never got over it, despite a peripatetic childhood that landed her in California.

She earned a Bachelor of Arts and a Master of Arts in English literature at UC Berkeley, raised a son, managed IT systems for a San Francisco law firm, and had a successful second career as a tutor for writing and Spanish—all the while working on her own writing.

Though she began as a poet, she loves complex historical stories that require a lot of research, and the events depicted in this account more than qualify. Her fictionalized account of the feud, *Before We Turn to Dust*, was published in the 2024 by Blue Handle Publishing.

Sneed and her husband split their time between Berkeley and Milam County, Texas.

WHAT TO READ NEXT

It's 1911 in the Texas Panhandle and Lena Snyder Sneed is madly in love. The only problem is, it's not with her husband Beal.

Beal Sneed, a cattle broker and rancher, is often away from their home in the wealthiest part of Amarillo, leaving Lena to care for the house and their two daughters.

And inadvertently to her own devices.

With Beal gone, Lena falls into an impassioned relationship with handsome bachelor Al Boyce Jr., another well-off cattleman and old family friend. And in the booming town of Amarillo, gossip spreads like wildfire, especially if it involves the rich.

When Beal gets wind of how far things have gone with Lena and Al, jealousy, revenge and pride brew up a Biblical storm that consumes three prominent families and leaves tragedy in its wake.

Based on one of the most infamous feuds in Texas history, and incorporating family archives, newspaper accounts and trial transcripts, *Before We Turn to Dust* is an honest, shocking and masterfully written glimpse into sex, society and justice in early 20th century Texas.